Note for Librarians: A cataloguing record for this book is available from Library and Archives
Canada at www.collectionscanada.ca/amicus/index-e.html
ISBN 1-4120-9075-x

PUBLISHING™
Offices in Canada, USA, Ireland and UK

Book sales for North America and international:
Trafford Publishing, 6E–2333 Government St.,
Victoria, BC V8T 4P4 CANADA
phone 250 383 6864 (toll-free 1 888 232 4444)
fax 250 383 6804; email to orders@trafford.com
Book sales in Europe:
Trafford Publishing (UK) Limited, 9 Park End Street, 2nd Floor
Oxford, UK OX1 1HH UNITED KINGDOM
phone 44 (0)1865 722 113 (local rate 0845 230 9601)
facsimile 44 (0)1865 722 868; info.uk@trafford.com
Order online at:
trafford.com/06-0831

10 9 8 7 6 5 4 3

Dedication

This book is dedicated to my father, the late John R. Roberts, who gave me the values and beliefs I hold today. He was deeply loved and highly respected; a man who made a huge impact on others through his own gentle leadership.

Acknowledgements

I would like to thank the numerous people who have helped in the creation of this book, starting with the extraordinary leaders everywhere who I've had the pleasure of working with for many years. They showed through their examples, how great leadership could transform the working environment for so many people.

I am deeply grateful to Dee van Straaten for once again providing me with her creative insight. Dee's happy disposition, bright smile and laughter made working through the graphic selection process so much more enjoyable. Her talents gave this book its cover, the layout and all of the fine chapter headings.

Thanks also go to Robyn, my youngest daughter who endured long evenings without my company and still encouraged me to keep working to bring the book to print.

I am greatly indebted to my family and friends who read the manuscript, provided feedback and encouraged me to put in the hours to bring this book to print. They are too numerous to mention but in particular I'd like to thank Chris Edley, Claude Maurice, Helen Martin and Cindy Lundy who provided feedback and many potential titles for consideration. To all of the people and who asked, cajoled, and encouraged me to keep writing – thank you for your persistent reminders and your belief in this endeavor.

Finally, I am indebted to the outstanding editing services of Eddy Piasenten. His careful attention to detail and valuable feedback helped to make this book a reality. His thoughtful suggestions encouraged me to re-write sections so that the important messages were so much clearer.

Introduction

For the past 26 years I have worked with leaders in a variety of organizations throughout North America and the United Kingdom. In the course of consulting within these organizations I've had the pleasure of working alongside many respected, highly effective leaders, each exhibiting their own unique style.

In my experience it would appear that some leaders **are** born to the role, while others have come to be highly respected through exposure to some dynamic and well-educated employees, coaches and mentors and through the participation in numerous and varied learning opportunities.

The leaders who have what appears to be a natural or ingrained way of working with people, people we call "born" leaders, seem to have demonstrated those leadership qualities fairly early in life. Research has shown that many have been involved in some form of leadership, formally or informally, long before reaching the workplace. Often their expertise in working with others was gained through volunteer work, by coaching youth or through initiatives commenced as students while still in high school. Perhaps their leadership aptitude emerged and was strengthened while coaching sports or by participating with family on home-based projects. Even having a paper route or lemonade stand might have contributed to the sense of responsibility and commitment to both the people and the job.

This does not mean to say that if you missed out on those opportunities in your formative years, you can't be a good leader. Just as many people have developed strong leadership qualities after entering the workplace and continued to develop their expertise through a willingness to modify their behavior. They may have developed their skills by working with dynamic leaders, ultimately recognizing that there are a variety of ways to obtain results and by applying new approaches and modifying them over time.

When working with leaders who have a strong commitment to their staffs' success, there appears to be some common belief systems – their core values. These include a belief in the value of the work they have chosen to do and in their employees. They believe that people generally want to make a great contribution and that it's important to have strong financial controls and a strategic plan with both long and short-term goals. This focus on their core values guides their choices, their actions and enables them to work with people in a more secure manner with a commitment to the long haul.

These leaders believe in people and their inherent good; that people want to make a positive contribution, to know categorically they have made a difference. They see beyond obstacles to opportunities – that doing better is always a possibility, that their people will want to join them in making a difference – and take steps to enact their beliefs. Probably their most important quality is that they listen as though their life depended on it. They hunger to learn, and ask deep, probing questions. They are passionate about celebrating; end results and work in progress, providing challenging opportunities and in creating an environment where people learn, grow and are rewarded for their contributions. They put others' well being, including both physical and emotional safety, high on their list of priorities. Above all they lead in a manner that models what they expect of others. They truly do lead by example.

In this book you will find examples from some of the best leadership activities and behaviors I've observed firsthand in the working world. You will also learn how small, often overlook things, can take leaders down paths that result in poor morale and hostile working relationships. Some of the best examples have come from small, privately run companies with a handful of employees while others come from multi-national organizations with thousands of employees worldwide. Some are from the retail world, from manufacturing, heavy industrial operations, the service sector, not-for-profit agencies and even Mom and Pop operations.

There are leadership styles from within Canada, the United States and the United Kingdom. Leaders' behaviors and personal styles vary from private, public and not-for-profit businesses and these different styles and approaches provide valuable lessons for leaders everywhere.

Some of the people you'll find in these pages have a 'fresh-faced' enthusiasm, an energy and passion fresh from college or university while others wear a timeworn expression that speaks of experience, results, changes and maturity. There are examples of leaders who continue to look for ways to improve their own working style; they strive to develop the people around them, and seem to constantly be considering ways to make yet another contribution, to apply a new approach, to leave a legacy, to know they have made a difference.

As you leaf through the pages you may recognize your own style in some of the activities, while some examples may trigger you to think of alternative approaches; places where you can make adjustments. For some of you there will be gentle reminders to go back to some of the things you once did so passionately but have since forgotten. For others there will be a fresh new concept on every page.

My hope is that this book will inspire you to try something new, to re-visit familiar but seldom-used approaches, and to re-connect with your people in ways that build skills, competence and confidence.

In these pages you'll find ways to make profound changes that can catapult your career upwards and inspire emerging leaders to make their own mark. If you act, and act carefully, following the concepts and examples from these pages, others will, in time, recognize your abilities because results will be more evident. You will find that your employees will become more courageous, more capable, more confident, and you will have made your mark as a leader worthy of the respect given by your employees, peers, superiors, even citizens of your community.

Read slowly, ponder long; proceed carefully. Be courageous, step forward, and try something new. Make certain that when you retire or move on to advance your own career, you leave behind highly skilled and capable employees because of your leadership and coaching.

How does this book work? It started one letter at a time which conjured up a thought and then a lesson, a memory of a leader and an example of the leadership in action. Each one could, and does stand alone; there is no pattern, no sequence, and no place to start or end.

Flip through the book in a random fashion, read a page a day, pick something that seems to "speak to you," or settle down for a journey into leadership development. The choice is yours.

There's something for everyone within these pages. Read, enjoy, reflect, apply and learn. A fresh new leader is just around the corner.

Table of Contents

ABC
DEFG
HIJK
LMNO
PQRS
TUVW
XYZ

Accountable

bound to give account, responsible, for things, to persons.

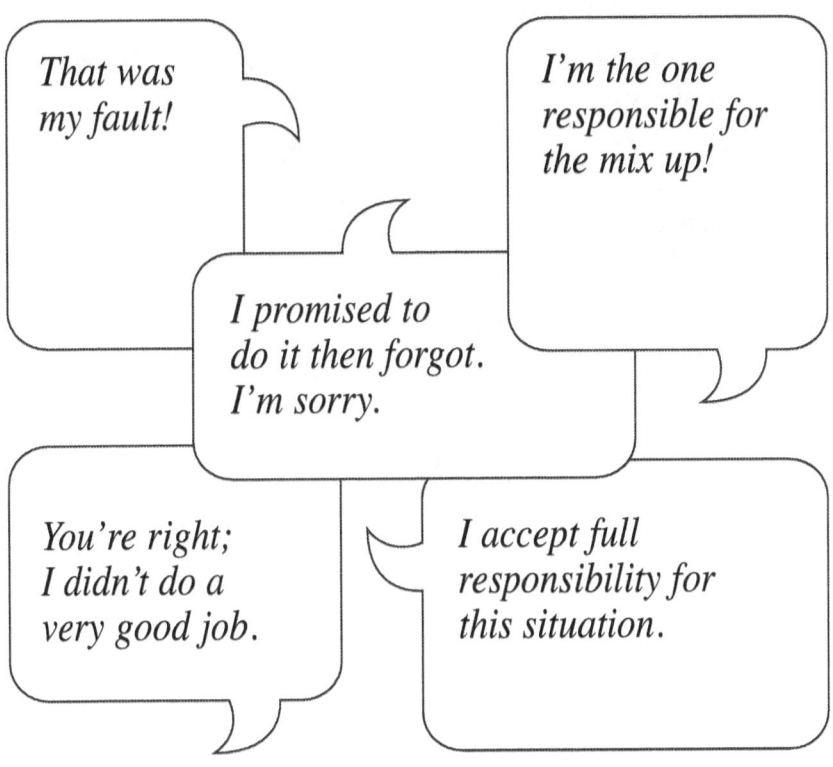

That was my fault!

I'm the one responsible for the mix up!

I promised to do it then forgot. I'm sorry.

You're right; I didn't do a very good job.

I accept full responsibility for this situation.

Accountability is a powerful quality. In the course of working with leaders in large, small, private, public and not-for-profit organizations one thing has stood out, time after time. Namely, the respect gained by leaders who admit their mistakes and accept responsibility for the outcomes.

These truly accountable leaders, even though somewhat circumspect and embarrassed, are willing to stand up and admit that their actions, judgments, business decisions or alliances have in part created the current situation.

These are the leaders who, when an error in judgment has been made, will openly talk about the line of thinking and the steps that led to some of their poorer decisions, and discuss and explore alternative directions that were not pursued. They strive to learn from mistakes, either their own, their peers or those of their employees, and use these occurrences as time for teaching and educating their staff. These leaders tend to move towards an exploration of the facts and data – the background steps – and away from individuals for blame or incrimination.

They seldom, if ever, seek to assign sole responsibility or punish the perpetrator of any errors in judgment.

Yet, in spite of all the obvious gains to be made, as honorable, moral, trustworthy individuals, unfortunately many leaders still strive to redirect attention to others. They justify the result, distance themselves from others, declare it wasn't important or even deny their involvement at all! Read the newspaper or watch the evening news and you'll find more than one leader abdicating responsibility. In some instances full blown corruption is under investigation and the leaders are adamantly declaring their innocence in spite of overwhelming facts to the contrary.

It's amazing to find juvenile, "it wasn't me," or "he/she did it," or "I wasn't the only one," playground language in boardrooms filled with senior vice presidents, executives and other seasoned veterans of the business world. Many of these leaders have MBAs and years of experience in boardrooms throughout the world, yet these same leaders, who talked openly, passionately about vision, codes of ethics and the need for transparency in their business transactions, violate their own guidelines time and again!

Why, you ask, would these experienced leaders, who have attained

heatherconsults@shaw.ca **L**is for **Leader**

positions of power, have completed years of university education, have built up strong and vibrant businesses and who have clambered up each one of the many corporate rungs, fail in this basic leadership quality?

The failure, in part, arises from the belief of shareholders, employees, customers, employers and peers that the leaders, the board members, and the CEOs, **must** be infallible. Leaders in organizations have proven time and again that they mistakenly believe that people are looking to them to always have the right answers. They believe that others expect them to:

- **know what to do in all the tough situations**
- **show the way clearly with every obstacle well thought out**
- **act as if they personally have the road map to business success**
- **prove their worth, as if their personal decisions will make or break the company single-handedly**

The assumptions are that as these individuals have risen to positions of power, are able to influence the direction of the organization, and are paid handsomely for the decisions they make, that they are going to make the right call time and again. People, forgetting these leaders are human, expect perfection and precision.

So, often acting alone, or trusting only a few key advisors, they step forward and make the business decisions that are indeed expected of them, the ones that will frequently thrust them into the limelight. When these seasoned, intelligent, educated people make a bad call, there is a natural tendency to deflect the focus away to avoid the media glare. "Don't look at me, look at the circumstances," they will say. "See the budget cuts I've had to deal with." "If only the competition hadn't launched their product ahead of us." "If only we didn't have the union to deal with." "If the president would only…"

While these might all be valid points, to dwell on them is counter-productive. It's far better to acknowledge the steps that were taken, to accept the current situation then look towards the future to explore new avenues to rectify the problem, implement some damage control or compensate innocent parties.

In order to build a reputation for yourself as an ethical and honorable leader you will need to operate in a careful manner, one open to scrutiny and examination.

The leader who is truly accountable will own their part in the situation, will accept the limits and lack of flexibility within the organization and still step boldly forward with some next steps dialogue.

The Accountable Leader will say:

- *In hindsight my decision has cost the company significantly and I regret that we will have to curtail some of the expansion plans we had for this quarter.*
- *Given that I was slow to approve the launch, and the competition beat us to market, let's look at what we can do to...*
- *As we have a strong union to work with, I will need to make sure they are included as partners with us on this. How do you recommend we proceed?*
- *Since I missed the deadline...*
- *Because I made a bad call on that product...*
- *As I was the one who decided to buy...*
- *I didn't see it coming.*
- *I regret it occurred; what are our options for moving forward?*

In other words the accountable leader acknowledges the situation or circumstances facing them, and, if appropriate, discloses and owns their personal role in creating part of the problem. They then step right into what actions are required to rectify the situation, ensuring that the future is brighter and an improvement is predicted.

This type of accountability has a huge spin-off throughout the rest of the organization. As other people see this example of leadership, it almost entirely removes fear – the fear of being penalized, ridiculed and held up for example. And as we all know, fear stifles creativity and growth and eliminates the courage to act.

If fear of failure is removed, if punishment is eliminated, if ridicule is stamped out, then people *will go out on a limb* to try to improve the ways in which they do business.

By showing it's okay to make errors – by accepting the part you, as the leader, have played – it goes a long way to creating strong, highly regarded leaders.

A story about Accountability

T he principal, the leader in a small independent school, made some financial decisions that backfired, almost putting the school out of business. As soon as the troubles became obvious, she met with the parents to explain what had happened, as they wanted to know how the school was going to recover.

At this meeting, with board members and teachers present, she openly declared she'd been the one to push for the financial decision that created the disaster. This principal went on to answer questions, deal with attacks on her management ability, and, when asked, said she was not leaving as she had a job to do. She told them she wanted to get the school back on a solid footing.

She then asked the parents for their trust and support in moving forward. She said she'd need them to work with her to help the school recover. She wanted them to keep their children at the school; in fact, she needed them to keep their children there in order to pay the bills.

There was a short pause and then one by one parents stood up to say, "you can count on me." Yes, she lost some of the students, and there were tough questions about the future and her ability to lead them forward but the vast majority stayed. Conversations in the corridors followed a common thread regarding the parent's decisions to support the principal.

"She's ethical and honest and is a perfect role model for our kids."

In time the school became stronger, enrolment not only stabilized it increased, and the school became known primarily for its ethical, values-driven leadership and the outstanding young citizens that emerged.

A B C
D E F G
H I J K
L M N O
P Q R S
T U V W
X Y Z

Boundaries

The real or understood line marking limit.

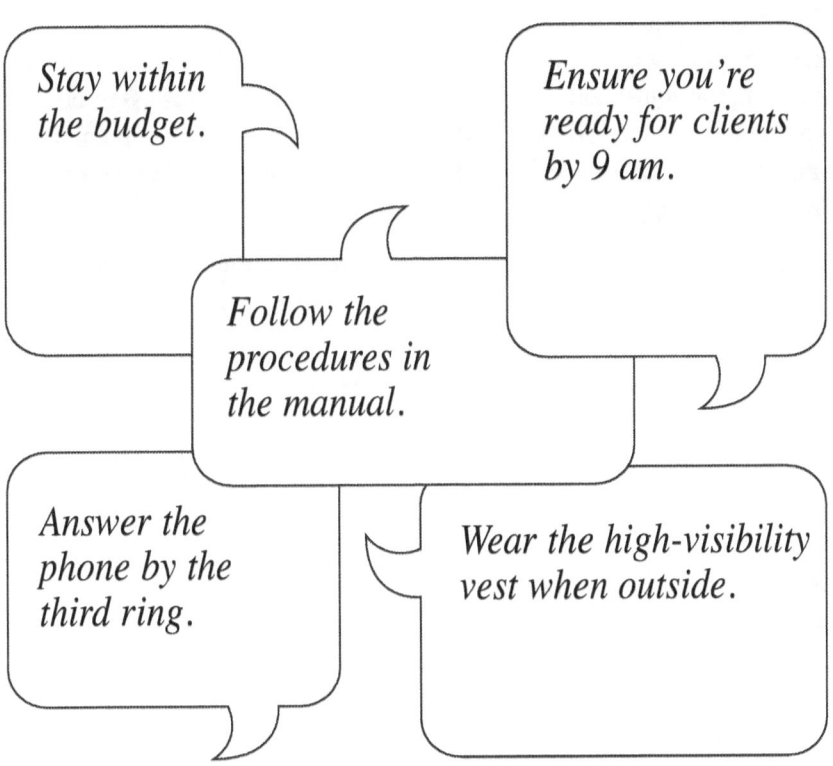

Stay within the budget.

Ensure you're ready for clients by 9 am.

Follow the procedures in the manual.

Answer the phone by the third ring.

Wear the high-visibility vest when outside.

B oundaries free people up to get on with the job. Yet a surprising number of leaders think it's up to the employee to figure out the right thing to do and just do it. *"After all, I hired adults; they shouldn't need to be told everything."* is a common refrain.

When you ask employees what they are expected to do, many will reply:

- Provide top notch customer service.
- Create an interesting window display.
- Be cost effective.
- Keep the warehouse well stocked.
- Make sure the account receivables are up to date.

When asked, *"what does top notch looks like?"* or *"what does an interesting display looks like?"* or *"how can you tell if you're being cost effective?"* or even *"what does a well-stocked warehouse look like?"* employees frequently stumble and have difficulty explaining the specific requirements. Without clarity, they also have no way of knowing if they are on track; they can't conduct a self-evaluation or make minor adjustments in their work. So, as a leader, it is essential your employees are provided with the boundaries that enable them to proceed with confidence. To know what boundaries look like we need to go back a few years!

As a child, most of us were given boundaries by our parents. They were clear, specific, could often be observed, and gave us a solid understanding of what was expected of us.

- *You may play outside as long as I can see you from the kitchen window.*
- *You must call me as soon as you get to your friend's home.*
- *Your bedroom must be tidied up. That means hanging up all of your clothes and putting the dirty things in the hamper.*
- *Be home by 10 o'clock.*
- *You may use the car if you fill the tank before you bring it back.*

You get the idea.

So, why is it that when leaders work with adults, they somehow think that providing boundaries is an inappropriate step? How wrong.

One of the key factors that influences the performance of employees is their ability to know and understand exactly what is required of them.

Someone has to tell them! It won't happen by osmosis!

Leaders who take the time to explain exactly what they want people to do and how they want it done, followed by a question or two to determine if there is anything that will prevent them from doing it that way, will find things go much more smoothly. This is in direct contrast to simply hoping they "understand without being told."

Boundaries provide security. Employees can make better decisions and will generally feel more confident. Confident employees tend to be happier and will be better positioned to provide great service to others – quite an important and significant ripple effect.

As a leader you have the opportunity to set boundaries; to create the framework for people to do their job. In some cases these boundaries can be established in conjunction with your staff. Imagine asking:

- *How many times is it reasonable for the phone to ring before you answer it?*
- *How often should the inventory be checked so we can re-order on time?*
- *When should be verify the data?*

Keep in mind, however, that most boundaries are not rigid, single points. There's usually some degree of flexibility. For example, starting work at 9:00 am may be a "start work boundary" but you would hardly expect the employee to stand outside until exactly 8:59 am before entering the workplace. A "clear the tables right after the customer has left" boundary may be within one minute most of the time or three if the restaurant is very busy.

The only times where absolute, pinpointed boundaries are demanded and expected are in cases of health and safety, and other areas where precision is essential. Some examples might be in surgery, at an airport, in a nuclear plant or any other highly critical scenarios where life and death situations arise.

The graph below shows a boundary with a tolerance range – the two lines.

As you see, most employees operate within the range most of the time, with a few exceptions.

A *someone who has gone beyond expectations*

B *someone whose performance has slipped below normal*

C *your typical employee*

Range of Acceptable Performance

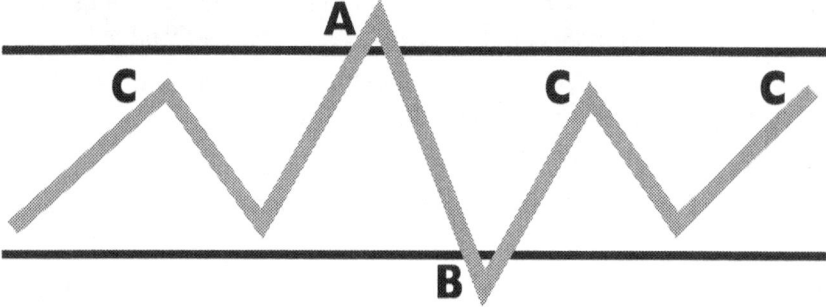

Most employees will operate within your tolerance range if it has been explained to them. If the employee knows that the reports have to be delivered to accounting by the 15th of each month, they will most likely meet that deadline. The accountant who knows she has until the afternoon break to complete a task will most likely work towards that deadline. The supervisor who knows they have until the middle of the month to submit their safety report will plan their time to meet that goal.

As leader, it is your responsibility to ensure staff at all levels know exactly what you expect of them and to set boundaries so they can proceed in confidence knowing how their work will be assessed.

Setting boundaries includes asking:
- **What needs to be done?**
- **How it is to be done?**
- **Who else might be involved?**
- **Where is the work to take place?**
- **What does a quality job looks like?**
- **When must it be completed?**

A story about Boundaries

A supervisor was concerned about health and safety issues and set up some meetings to discuss ways to improve the working environment in the open-pit mine. The employees came together with their records of incidents and accidents, local safety regulations and a list of ideas that they felt could and should be implemented.

The leader, a skilled and respected facilitator, knew things could get out of hand very quickly and that important information could be lost if some boundaries were not established immediately. This leader also knew that to impose the boundaries on this experienced team would not be well received.

At the beginning of the meeting he reminded everyone that the goals for the meeting were to discuss key safety issues, determine possible strategies to minimize risks and improve the safety of everyone in the mine, and to work towards solutions that would be realistic given the financial constraints.

He then asked the team an important "boundary forming" question.

If we are going to run this meeting in an open, respectful way so that we get all of the ideas on the table, how will we need to interact during the meeting?

Immediately the participants came up with a list of things including:

- One person talks at a time.
- We make sure we get all of the issues on the table before we look for solutions.
- We won't engage in 'us and them' conversations – safety affects everyone.
- We should post the financial constraints on the board so we can be realistic.
- We agree that every idea is valuable as it may trigger other thoughts.

The leader recorded the "boundaries" on a flip chart and posted them on the wall. The meeting then proceeded and all of the participants worked within the "boundaries" they had set for themselves.

Occasionally one of the participants would stop the meeting to draw attention to the fact that they were not following their own boundaries and that they needed to get back within their guidelines.

A very productive and valuable meeting resulted with people feeling their ideas had been heard and respected. The time it took to set the boundaries was minimal. Yet, it meant the leader was able to focus on the content, to listen to the people, and had to devote less effort to the process.

ommunication

Impart, transmit, share, act of imparting information, to make others understand one's ideas, to be in touch by word or signals, a sending, giving, or exchanging information.

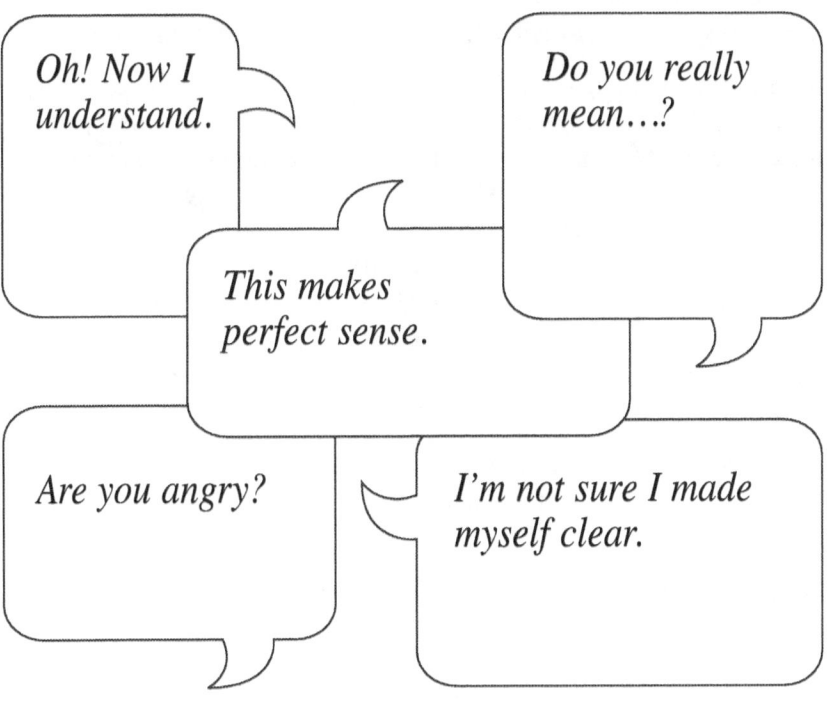

Oh! Now I understand.

Do you really mean…?

This makes perfect sense.

Are you angry?

I'm not sure I made myself clear.

C lear, precise communication is important. I have heard it said that we have two eyes, two ears and one mouth and that we should use them in that order!

In surveys on the topic of communication employees always say they want more – more communication, more information on a regular basis, more information that's useful and timely. The biggest complaint employee's have is about being kept in the dark, of not being informed of changes that have the potential to alter their habitual way of working.

On top of that, while it's nice to hear the CEO's speech or the President chat with employees, they really want the information directly from the person they report to. Research shows that most employees perceive their front-line supervisor, leader or manager as being in a position to honestly give them the "straight goods." This person is generally considered to be far less concerned with politics and more connected to the reality of the work.

Communicating is about transmitting information so that it is received and understood as it was intended. This can be accomplished in any number of ways and often leads to misinterpretation. The challenge then is to find a way to convey content and meaning without distortion.

So is talking – giving out information – really what communicating is all about? While it's certainly a part of it, it's by far the smallest part; there's a great deal more to communicating than simply talking. In fact, when it comes to believing information, the verbal content has only a small impact on our willingness to accept and believe the information. The visual message plays the most significant part in the entire communication process. What individuals select to wear, their age, cleanliness, gender, facial expressions, accessories, mannerisms, and on and on are the keys to believability. These things "speak" much louder than anything that is said.

Before we look at the actual verbal message, it's important to pause long enough to examine the thought processes that lead to the outward message, because that's where it all originates.

What you THINK about the information you have to convey and what you THINK about the person, to whom you will be speaking, is transmitted non-verbally. No matter what the leader WANTS the person to believe, if he or she doesn't believe it, it will become transparent. If the leader doesn't trust the person, that will become evident, too. You can practice the speech or hone your verbal skills, but first you must ask yourself:

- **Do I believe this?**
- **Is it true?**
- **Is this what I want to say?**
- **Will this person use the information wisely?**
- **Will this help?**
- **What do I really want to accomplish here?**

Once you are clear about your biases look at how to get your message across clearly and honestly, so that learning takes place.

First there's a complicated chain of mental events that rapid-fire through your head right before the verbal information is provided.

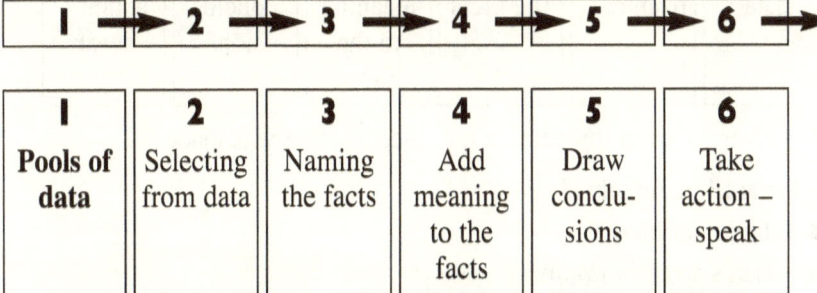

1	2	3	4	5	6
Pools of data	Selecting from data	Naming the facts	Add meaning to the facts	Draw conclu-sions	Take action – speak

I First of all, there is a pool of data available to choose from. For example, for an individual there are all manner of visible things to notice, including height, age, gender and appearance. There are accents, tones of voice, pace and urgency of their speech, and then there's the whole range of things they speak about, a variety of things they have said to combine the pool of data.

1	2	3	4	5	6
Pools of data	**Selecting from data**	Naming the facts	Add meaning to the facts	Draw conclusions	Take action – speak

2 Then there's the selection process.

What am I choosing to talk about?

- John is *not talking about the problem*.
- Susan's *report is incomplete*.
- Mary is *looking out of the window*.

1	2	3	4	5	6
Pools of data	Selecting from data	**Naming the facts**	Add meaning to the facts	Draw conclusions	Take action – speak

3 This is followed by naming the selection that was made.

What am I calling this?

- John is *indirect*,
- Susan's work is *sloppy*,
- Mary is *inattentive*.

1	2	3	4	5	6
Pools of data	Selecting from data	Naming the facts	**Add meaning to the facts**	Draw conclusions	Take action – speak

4 Following this is my opinion, beliefs and assumptions about the selection.

Is this important? Is it positive? Is it good, bad, responsible, distracting, harmful, helpful and so on.

- John is indirect and *this is wrong*.
- Susan's work was sloppy; *she must have been rushed*.
- Mary's more inattentive than usual; *I must be boring her*.

1	2	3	4	5	6
Pools of data	Selecting from data	Naming the facts	Add meaning to the facts	**Draw conclu-sions**	Take action – speak

5 Then, there are my conclusions.

- John *won't be receptive to this*.
- I bet *she will be glad to let me know about her workload*.
- I *better do something to make her sit up and pay attention*.

1	2	3	4	5	6
Pools of data	Selecting from data	Naming the facts	Add meaning to the facts	Draw conclu-sions	**Take action – speak**

6 Finally comes the action. This is where the actual words selected are strung together to present a point of view, to form the question, to seek clarification, etc.

- So, to John you might find yourself saying, *"I know you won't like what I have to say, but you need to be more direct and come right out and say what's on you mind."*
- To Susan you might say, *"You must have a lot on your plate these days as this work is sloppy; it's not up to your usual standard."*
- And for Mary, you might be tempted to say something outrageous just to jolt her, or you could find yourself saying, *"Clearly you'd rather be somewhere else. Is this boring you Mary?"*

Perhaps an even more astonishing fact is that the time-lapse between steps 1 and 6 can be measured in mere seconds. John, Susan and Mary, meanwhile, may be quite taken aback by these comments as they had not been privy to your thoughts.

Another way of looking at the communication process and the many potential breakdowns waiting to trip people up is by recalling a conversation with someone when you were unhappy or dissatisfied with the outcome.

Draw a line down the centre of a sheet of paper. Label one side "Dialogue" and record your recollection of the conversation. Label the other side "Thoughts" and try to recall what you were thinking, *but didn't talk about.*

Thoughts	Dialogue

Here's an example of what a simple communication process might look like.

Thoughts	Dialogue
I think, *John looks bored* So I say...	I said *"Why don't you go and finish the project you were working on."*
I think, *He'd rather sit here and not participate than do some real work,* so I say ...	He said *"I don't want to miss this topic."*
	I said *"That project is important and I can bring you up to speed on this later?"*
	He said *"Get off my case will you, I told you before I'd get it done on time"*
I think, *Gosh this is getting out of hand,* so I say ...	I said *"Suit yourself, but it better be done on time!"*

Now you have a true picture of the complexity of the communication process. Add to this your emotions, concerns, even your energy on that given day and you'll see that yet another layer of complexity has been added.

Finally, consider your history with that person. Has it been positive, or are there some old feuds lingering to color the conversation?

As you can see, there's a lot of second guessing going on as each person is busy making rapid assumptions about what the other person is thinking. The interesting point to consider is that the other person has his or her own thoughts – their own "sheet of paper," – just like this one, and generally, neither is shared openly. How much better it would be to ask for more information or to reveal our own thinking as we go along.

The more-effective leaders use both advocacy and enquiry to drill down on issues so they truly learn and can make better decisions. They generally use a "check in" process to see if their message has been understood, is valid or complete. They want and need to make sure their information is "comprehended as transmitted," to find out if there is something missing from the point of view they presented. They also want to gain clarity from those who speak to them, to truly understand by seeking more information.

In addition to advocating their point of view they are strong proponents of using enquiry with this approach. The two go hand-in-hand; they provide their point of view, and provide background information or experience to add validity to their perspective **and** they ask for feedback on their opinions, in essence asking others to help them see their "blind spots".

Advocacy (with background information and/or enquiry) includes statements like:

- *I believe it will be helpful to… that worked at… can you help me see what I might have missed?*
- *I would like to… as I believe …. Can you add anything to this line of thinking?*
- *My experience with… leads me to suggest we do… what are your thoughts?*
- *I'd like to initiate… we did it at… but I'd like to hear where this might cause a problem.*
- *If we proceed with my idea, what are the biggest issues our staff will have?*
- *I would like to… because… can you provide two or three opposing points of view, things that I might have missed?*

Enquiry includes statements like:

- *Help me understand why... is important?*
- *How would... save us money?*
- *Where could we get... to help us move forward with the project?*
- *Why do you believe that would be useful?*
- *Can you explain how it made a difference last time?*
- *Can you think of anything I might have missed?*
- *I'm not sure I've thought of everything; can you show me what might make this idea stronger?*
- *From your point of view how could we make things safer?*
- *What are you thinking that leads you to say...?*
- *What assumptions are you making that causes you to say...?*

In other words, these leaders care about being heard accurately, and hearing others accurately too. They don't believe they "have *the* answers" even when they willingly put forward their ideas. They want, demand, and actively seek people to challenge their perspectives, thereby contributing to a better solution or idea. These leaders **do not** want **"Yes"** people! They want people who will help them be better leaders and make better decisions.

Thank you for providing another point of view.

That was a very helpful exchange of ideas.

I'm glad you pointed that out; I missed that potential problem.

Will you help me go over some of the possibilities, as I'm sure I'm missing something important?

This is an example of the previous conversation with the addition of some advocacy and enquiry. You'll notice there's a substantial difference in how the conversation proceeds with that additional information.

Thoughts	Dialogue
I think *John looks bored* So I say…	I said *"This doesn't seem to be particularly relevant to you John. Why don't you go back to that project you were working on before the meeting."* He said *"I don't want to miss this topic."*
I think *He'd rather sit here and not participate than do some real work,* so I say …	I said *"I know you don't want to miss it, but this is not something you can contribute to and I'm concerned about the deadline we have for the XYJ project. It's important to get it done and I can bring you up to speed on this later. Can you tell me why staying here is the best use of your time?"* He said *"Don't be so persistent, I told you before I'd get it done on time, and I want to hear what Bill has to say."*
I think *Gosh, this is getting out of hand,* so I say …	I said *"I am being persistent because, I need that project completed today. Let's meet later this afternoon when I can bring you up to speed on what Bill had to report."*

Finally, the leader who cares about getting things right, wants to confirm that the communication was understood as intended. They do this by paraphrasing – feeding back the essence of the information.

You might recognize this from people who say, "Let me see if I understand the issue. You are saying…." Or "So the problem is… is that right?" They feed back enough to show they were listening and that they care about accuracy.

A story about Communication

A supervisor in a government agency was struggling to develop a solid working relationship with her manager. Time and again they were at cross-purposes. Decisions were delayed, more facts had to be provided, others had to be consulted before action could be taken. Then the supervisor sought out a coach to help her find the root cause of the mis-communication. In time, and after looking at the background sheets the supervisor had filled in from conversations that had gone awry, they were able to identify some key areas where she would be able to make progress.

Together, they identified a basic communication-style difference and that, by making some adaptations, the supervisor could "manage" her boss more effectively.

The supervisor realized her manager needed more time to digest facts before making a decision. Their past meetings showed a history of postponing decisions until the manager had had sufficient time to review the facts and weigh the options. Clearly the manager was a reflective listener, averse to risk and as such needed some quiet time to consider the facts and weigh the consequences.

Armed with this simple observation the supervisor started providing background data in advance of their meetings so the manager could prepare. They were then able to proceed more smoothly and reach decisions far quicker than they had in the past.

For more on Communication, see the topics, "OPEN", "INVOLVE" "QUESTIONS" AND "FEEDBACK"

Demonstrate

Show, describe and explain by help of specimens or experiments, to show clearly and openly by action.

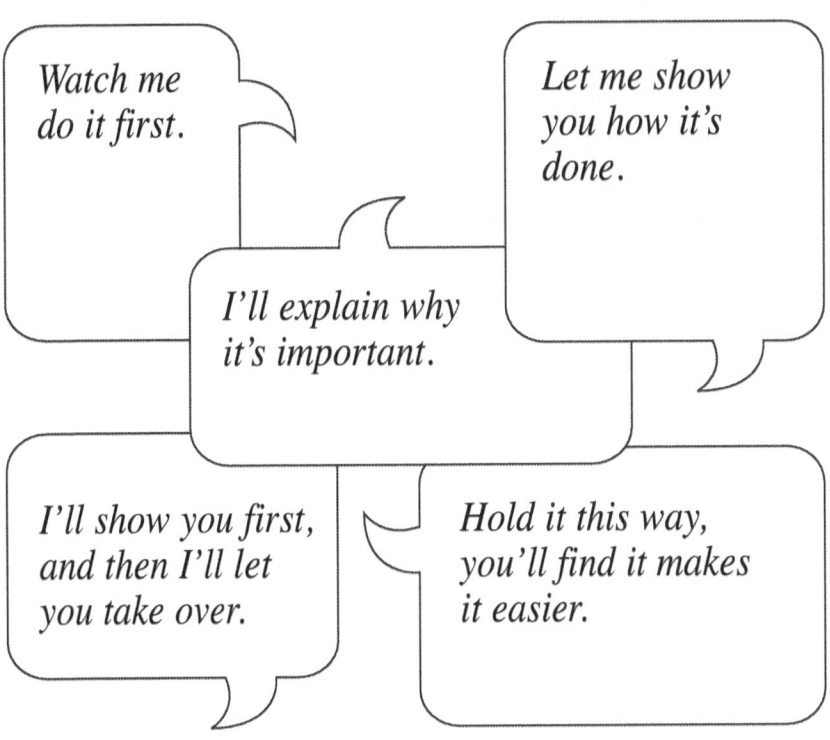

Watch me do it first.

Let me show you how it's done.

I'll explain why it's important.

I'll show you first, and then I'll let you take over.

Hold it this way, you'll find it makes it easier.

D edicated leaders want other people to be successful; generally they derive a great deal of satisfaction from seeing others develop their skills, gain knowledge, become more and more competent and exude confidence. To ensure their staff grow and develop, they teach, they coach, they fine tune and they give feedback. Perhaps most important, is their willingness to show others the ropes, their own special approach, and techniques, by modeling the right way.

Everyone learns by examining and studying others. Great musicians, fine painters, extraordinary scientists and strong leaders all began by modeling their actions after others. In time they found their own style, their own voice so to speak and will in turn be followed by others.

Leaders who want their staff to be successful take the time to think through the complete learning cycle.

- They consider the task that needs to be done.
- They consider the person who will complete the work.
- They determine the gap between the employee's present ability and the requirements of the job.

Coaching leaders ask themselves many questions long before they commence the training process:

- *What do I want this person to do?*
- *How knowledgeable are they right now?*
- *What opportunities have they had to practice?*
- *What reference materials are available to them?*
- *How often will they be required to do this?*
- *How interested are they in developing their expertise?*
- *How can I help them see value in becoming more proficient?*
- *What advantages exist for this employee if they master this?*
- *What time will be required to provide a solid understanding of the requirements?*
- *What are the barriers to becoming highly competent?*
- *What time will it take for this novice to become able to work alone?*

And so on.

Once these questions have been answered, the effective leader looks inward and asks some more:

- *Am I the best person to demonstrate what I'm looking for?*
- *Am I certain I can show what I want?*
- *Can I articulate the process and steps in a clear manner?*
- *What resources will I need to do this well?*
- *What support will I be able to provide as they gain expertise?*

Once some in-depth analysis has been completed, the leader considers the basic learning principles which must be applied when working with adults. Trainers, coaches and instructors use these principles whenever they are helping adults learn new skills as they provide a framework for the learning experience. This is a well-known maxim amongst business communicators which has a strong application to a variety of training situations.

Tell them what you're going to tell them.
(This is an overview of what's going to take place)

Tell them.
(This is when you do just what you said you'd do)

Tell them what you told them.
(This is a summary of the key elements from the training event)

Another recognized training guideline that's worth remembering and applying is:

As an individual engaged in learning...

I hear and I forget.
(The result when the instructor only talks about the topic)

I see and I remember.
(Showing makes a stronger impact; people retain the information)

I do and I understand.
(A hands-on opportunity solidifies the true requirements and complexity of completing a task)

When adults are learning they benefit from a simple show-and-tell process, as recognized by the many "do it yourself" TV programs.

The leader has to decide if they are the best person to provide the demonstration or if there is another more skilled and knowledgeable person who can take on the task. In some cases, the leader may ask another employee to give the demonstration and training so that this person can gain skills in conducting training and providing demonstrations.

Whatever choice is made, the leader's primary goal is to ensure the trainee is more capable after the demonstration and training.

The following model shows the learning curve of a trainee/trainer relationship.

High	Highly supportive – interested in hearing new ideas Listens, discusses, considers Willing to adapt – try new things Gives freedom to make adjustments – fine tunes Provides little direction allows independent thinking and action **3**	Provides a high degree of direction Coaches – provides tips and techniques Empathizes with trainee as they strive to master new skills Makes sure trainee is not too hard on themselves Encourages – gives feedback – supports efforts – cheerleads **2**
Two-way communication	Delegates authority – shows confidence Asks for deadlines – trusts employee to meet goals Provides almost no direction – employee owns the job Holds individual accountable Reviews result acknowledges accomplishments	Provides details about job – both the how and why Explains the process – step by step Little freedom until basics mastered Trains extensively – stays close at hand to help if needed Provides feedback often – catches the right things, corrects errors before they become habits.
Low	**4**	**1**
	High	Experience to the task at hand	Low

Across the bottom you'll notice there is low experience on the right with high experience on the left.

At the top there is a high probability for two-way interaction and an exchange of ideas and at the bottom more of an emphasis on one way directive communication.

The path to learning starts in Quadrant 1 and continues until the trainee has reached Quadrant 4.

Quadrant One

- Starting here the leader acts according to this quadrant. The amount of detail provided is directly related to the experience of the trainee. Clear step by step points are made and the rationale is made explicit. Constant feedback is an essential element.

Quadrant Two

- By the time the trainees is at the second stage, the leader will be providing less direct information and giving more freedom to work alone, while encouraging and supporting efforts to become masterful. Empathy becomes more important as the new trainees are often disillusioned by their slow progress.

Quadrant Three

- By now the trainee is experienced enough to bring forward alternate approaches and new ideas and usually wants some flexibility from the leader. The leader will demonstrate an interest in hearing new ideas and will be more inclined to say, "let's try it out," allowing the trainee to test their ideas and validate the new approach

Quadrant Four

- Finally the trainee is no longer learning very much about this task, but is considered a seasoned and experienced employee, able to make independent decisions and to execute the task without intervention from the leader.

So, as a leader, find out if you're doing a great job of demonstrating by answering these questions:

- *Have I been showing my staff different ways to handle aspects of the work?*
- *Do I make my own approaches transparent so they can learn from me?*

- *Have I engaged others more fully so they can gain expertise?*
- *Have I created and do I follow a systematic training plan for my staff?*
- *Are my people becoming more and more skillful as a result of working with me?*

A story about Demonstrating

A young man was going to start work in a warehouse. His job would require him to lift pallets loaded with bales of pulp and pack them into railcars. He had never operated a forklift before and, while having a tour, appeared intimidated by the speed of operation by some of the more experienced employees. His supervisor wanted to put him at ease, and ensure he understood the safe operation of the forklift and how to work in the confined space of the railcar.

When the young man arrived for work the next day, he was surprised to find the supervisor wanted to meet with him away from the job site. When they met he found the supervisor had arranged for a senior forklift operator to join them. The supervisor explained that they had set up a mock site for training purposes and this other man was going to be his trainer. The supervisor also explained that while he, himself, could run the forklift from time to time, he wasn't the most skilled at explaining the finer details that would be used every day.

The supervisor explained how he wanted the training to take place and asked the senior trainer if he could see any problems with proceeding as outlined. They then discussed and agreed on the plan.

The whole day was devoted to watching forklift training films and observing the drivers on the floor, followed by on-site demonstrations and hands-on practice sessions. The young man reported he'd never anticipated that so much time would be devoted to driving a forklift. He appreciated the fact that his supervisor had found him an experienced operator to conduct the training and that he'd followed a carefully prepared and comprehensive plan.

At the end of the week the young man was seen operating the forklift like a pro. His confidence was evident: he was seen driving, loading, reversing and un-loading pulp into railcars in a careful and conscientious manner. The supervisor pointed him out to us and spoke about the progress he'd made. The supervisor then gave him the "thumbs up" before returning to his office.

This operation earned an award in 2002 for its outstanding safety record. We don't need to wonder why.

ABCDEFGHIJKLMNOPQRSTUVWXYZ

Empowering

To delegate legal power to, authorize, to enable.

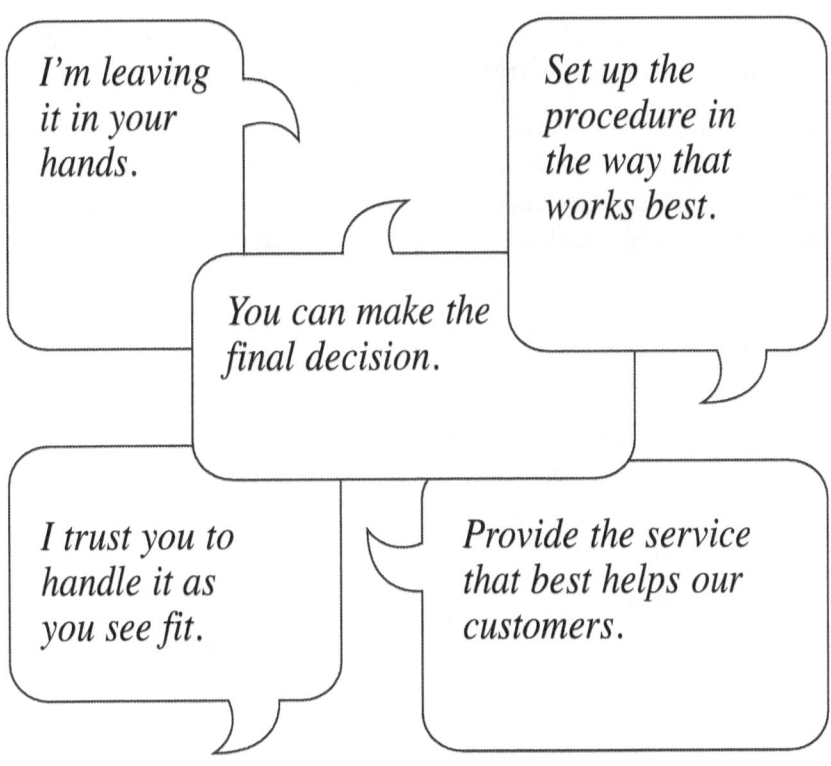

I'm leaving it in your hands.

Set up the procedure in the way that works best.

You can make the final decision.

I trust you to handle it as you see fit.

Provide the service that best helps our customers.

E mpowered individuals make things happen. Leaders often wish employees would make decisions, do what it takes to get the job done and not forever wait for someone to tell them what to do in any given situation. Leaders would like it if their employees would use their own judgment when there is not a clear and straightforward "rule" or "policy" to follow. Yet time and again employees hesitate; come for direction or they stand fast behind the policy or rule when clearly the situation calls for an exception to be made.

So, what is empowerment and how can you recognize it in the workplace? What makes it an empowered act and not a reckless disregard for sound business practices?

When employees make independent decisions, adjust procedures, make amendments to existing plans, authorize payments, or respond to customer's concerns by making an unusual decision, or fine-tuning a policy, while upholding the principles and values of the organization, they are, empowered employees.

The ability to act, to call the shots, to decide Yes or No is powerful indeed. But, what environment allows the employee this degree of freedom?

First and foremost, the leader has, over time, usually provided more and more freedom to act based on the past performance of this employee. And the employee knows that their leader has seen them in action, trusts their decisions and respects their problem-solving and critical-thinking processes.

It's generally a well-trained, experienced employee who is likely to be found acting in an empowered manner. Over time they have come to trust the working style of their leader, to know what is likely to be approved or not, and understand the degree to which they can step away from the normal path. They have worked with the leader to establish and work within boundaries and know what might constitute an acceptable "exception."

So, when the "empowered" employee is faced with a dilemma, they act – they make the decision, they consider the result, weigh the cost and make the final call.

Once the decision has been made, the employee will usually meet with the leader to explain what occurred and their line of thinking that led to the decision. They make sure they keep their leader informed so there are no surprises.

So what does the leader do to create this belief in their ability to make these decisions?

At what point do their employees say to themselves, "I will make the decision that I believe is appropriate, I do not need to get approval, I do not need to wait, and I can act right now."

To get to this stage the leader has, in all likelihood, engaged in group problem solving and brainstorming sessions so employees can explore options, consider the ripple effect and appreciate the ramifications of their choices. In addition, the leader has usually made their own decision-making transparent so employees can see how they make decisions. They "think out loud," so to speak, so others gain insight into their line of thinking.

Leaders who believe it's essential to have empowered employees typically provide far more information than their counterparts. They "open the book" and talk about business issues, financial matters and shareholder concerns. In fact their employees often provide the numbers and can see them un-altered when the leader presents them in reports. There is an exchange of information and both leaders and employees can rely on the information.

These leaders make a conscious effort to educate and inform their employees about many aspects of the business so they are equipped to make the necessary decisions when the circumstances demand it.

A story about Empowering

A vast, international forestry company, with operations throughout the globe, and with what could be termed a vociferous union, noticed some anomalies in the results their employees were creating. The vice presidents were noticing the exceptional results emerging from some operations and wanted to find out what was contributing to the improvements.

Safety in one operation was clearly head and shoulders above the "normal" performance of others in the same geographic area. The cost of road-building was halved in one operation, while in another employee relations were amazing as the people worked in harmony while creating high-quality products. Meanwhile production costs were significantly reduced at one paper machine.

The Vice Presidents were curious:

- **Why were they getting these improved results?**
- **What could be the source of these exceptional changes?**

I was one of a team of consultants brought in to un-cover the factors that led to these results.

One example directly related to empowerment. A blaster, working on some new roads, heard from a friend about some new inexpensive explosives. He ordered a sample to try out – empowered to buy!

The tests he carried out – empowered to try something new – provided mixed results. When the explosive was dry it was effective when wet it was useless. This employee asked the machine shop to fabricate a pump, so water could be pumped from the drill holes – empowered to request a peer to work on a special project. The machine shop agreed – more empowerment. The pump was fabricated, tested and proved highly effective. Empowerment continues!

The employee then placed a larger order of the explosive and devised a way to track the results and cost savings. After one month he prepared a brief presentation for the manager and the accounting department. This employee saved his division over $15,000 during one month.

The manager, when asked how all of this could have happened right under his nose, told us: *"I provide the employees with all the information they need to do the best job possible. I tell them to work efficiently and to save money wherever possible without sacrificing safety and our other key measures. Then I leave it up to them."*

After all of the results had been explored and the leadership styles had been identified, the company president brought together the leaders and the individual innovators who had made such a difference. At a two-day conference they celebrated and gave the employees an opportunity to share their various techniques and leadership styles. What a roomful of energy they created.

Feedback

The carrying back of some of the effects of some process to its source or to a preceding stage, so as to strengthen or modify it.

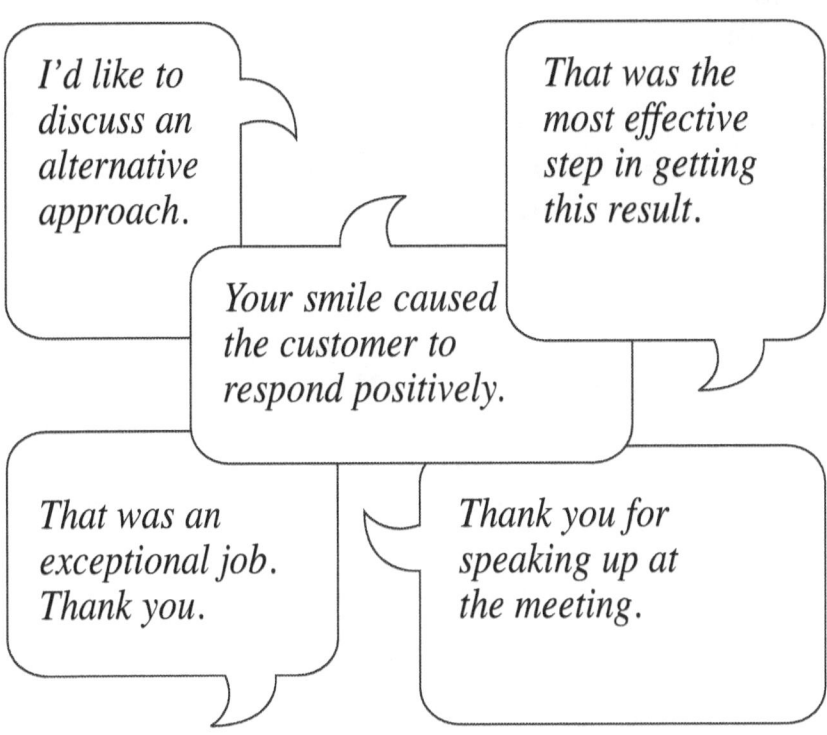

I'd like to discuss an alternative approach.

That was the most effective step in getting this result.

Your smile caused the customer to respond positively.

That was an exceptional job. Thank you.

Thank you for speaking up at the meeting.

F eedback is an essential leadership tool. Yet it's amazing how many employees talk about the lack of feedback they receive. They work diligently and make their contributions daily, weekly, monthly with little or no comment on their work. On the other hand, managers, supervisors and others in leadership roles often cringe at the thought of "having" to give feedback, as if this is something their employees don't want.

Feedback happens whether you've planned it of not. The trouble is the feedback that "just happens," the spontaneous, unplanned conversation can derail performance and lead to poor service and unhappy situations.

Effective leaders understand that feedback is essential to enhancing and re-directing individual performance. They view it as a gift, a caring provision of information that will enable someone to become stronger. They know the absence of feedback may actually slow progress as it can create doubt, or conversely, create unwarranted confidence and lead people to make inappropriate decisions. But above all, the lack of feedback makes employees feel invisible, as if nobody notices the contributions they make every day. The lack of timely feedback can ultimately lead to performance that slides and demands attention. But by then it might well be too late.

Some people are good at giving themselves feedback!

- *Hey, I did a great job on that project.*
- *I'm proud of the results I created.*
- *Not bad for my first attempt.*

My young granddaughter gave me a striking example of this when she was just three years old. Climbing up a hill near our home the terrain became very rough and steep. She was walking ahead of me so I could keep an eye on her and I overheard her chatting to herself. It went like this, "I can't do this. I can't do this." *While she kept putting one foot in front of the other,* "Oh! I'm doing it – well done Amy-Beth."

We then proceeded on along a flat section and on reaching another steep rise she repeated the same lines. "I can't do this. I can't do this." *A pause as she walked on.* "Oh! I'm doing it – well done Amy-Beth." once again she acknowledged that she was actually climbing the hill and praised herself.

Amy-Beth was noticing the challenge as well as her accomplishments and felt it was worth patting herself on the back. After listening to this self talk, I too gave her some words of praise that valued her commitment to stick with it even though it was a tough climb for her short legs. She in turn grinned at me and plodded on. At the end of the hike she rushed to talk to her Mom. "I made it all the way to the top," she said, with great pride.

So, feedback is an essential tool and it can be applied to high, low and consistent, reliable performers.

For the high performer it's about acknowledging their contributions. A simple *"Thank you"* can make all the difference and helps the person feel valued.

For the poorer performer it might be, *"I'm concerned about... let's talk."*

And for the reliable, consistent, dependable employee it might be, *"I can always count on you," "your consistent performance helps us reach our targets," "you're so reliable,"* or *"it's good that I know you're always on time."*

Many effective leaders use a "formula" for providing corrective feedback. This formula reminds them of what they want to accomplish, the process to engage the employee, and the follow-up required when everyone returns to work.

When an important change or correction is required, try this approach.

Note: it's important to do your homework **before** you talk with the employee.

1. Have the facts on the actual performance. What is this employee doing or not doing?
2. Obtain the facts on the expectations or standards for the job. What is expected? Was it communicated to the employee?
3. Identify the GAP. What am I getting or not getting?
4. Arrange to talk in private. "I'm concerned about... I'd like to discuss it with you. How about this afternoon at two?"

The Meeting

1. **Present** the information *"Our start time is 9 a.m. and I've noticed you have come in at 9:15 twice this week. I'm concerned about your punctuality"*.

2. **Ask** for the employee's perspective. *"Tell me what's causing you to be late?"*

3. **Confirm** you understand (paraphrase, and provide feedback to show you listened). Remember, you may or may not agree with what they say but you can show you've heard their point of view. *"So, you say your regular baby sitter is sick and your sister-in-law is helping out but she has to take a bus that is often late."*

4. **Ask** the employee for some ideas that could change the current performance. *"What other options have you explored that will allow you to get here for 9?"*

5. **Confirm** your understanding of their options. *"So, you're saying you haven't told your sister-in-law that you'd like her to catch the 8:15 bus."*

6. **Agree** on a solution(s) *"Okay, you're going to ask your sister-in-law to catch the bus at 8:15 tomorrow so you'll get here by 9. Your regular sitter is due back on Wednesday right? If you run into problems in the future let's talk, we may be able to work out a temporary change to your hours."*

7. **Establish** a follow-up date to assess progress. *"Check with me on Monday so I'll know if your sitter is able to return. If needed we can work out another arrangement."*

Feedback can be used when you would like some minor adjustment in a person's behavior. When you want to let someone know you value or appreciate some aspect of their behavior, ***and need a minor adjustment*** you can use a different approach.

- **Tell** them what you value, appreciate, admire, etc.
- **Ask** them to do more of something, or less of it.
- **Explain** how it helps you.
- **Ask** for their help.

Example: *"I really appreciated it when you spoke up at the meeting today and shared your point of view. I'd like you to do much more of that as it helps me really know the perspective of all of the team. Will you make an effort to do that more often?"*

Conversely: *"I really appreciated it when you spoke up at the meeting today and shared your point of view. I'd like it if you would work with me by holding on to your thoughts until I hear from some of our quieter members, so I hear everyone's perspective. Will you help me with this?"*

So remember, feedback is essential. Employees are looking for it. They not only want feedback, they need it, as it's essential for their growth. Your organization will become stale if contributions are not appreciated, fine tuned or modified significantly. Feedback is key to personal and business growth.

It only takes a few important minutes to build expertise and fine-tune performance.

Effective leaders know the value of saying:

- *I really like the way you handled that tough situation.*
- *I'm worried about... let's talk.*
- *Your skills have really developed. I saw the difference in how you worked with that client.*
- *I noticed... I'd like to discuss another approach.*
- *So you feel angry when... If I were in your shoes I'd probably be concerned too.*
- *You say your employees will be upset if we introduce.... How else might we solve the dilemma?*

A story about Feedback

I had been working in an automotive plant in the United Kingdom that had been pre-occupied with labour negotiations when it became apparent the employees were not only adamant that they were under-paid but more importantly unrecognized and under-valued as key players in the success of the operation.

The senior management team and a handful of consultants conducted a survey and found a significant number of employees made comments like:

I never hear a good word about the things I do to make this place stay in business.

All we get are complaints when a problem occurs.

When are we going to get some recognition for all of our hard work?

The senior management team talked with their managers, supervisors and team-leaders and discovered most of their interactions with the employees were about problems in production. Rather than being closeted away in their offices, they were indeed out on the production floor. They were highly visible and available to their employees, but the trouble was, their entire focus was on correcting the multitude of production, maintenance and service problems. Their energy and focus were on things that had gone wrong – so much so that they had forgotten about all the things that were going well, the things their employees had been addressing that had created a positive impact on the business.

Management agreed that while problems still had to be dealt with promptly there was an opportunity to provide feedback that recognized the outstanding work employees were doing which had been forgotten with the problem-solving focus.

Each of the managers, supervisors and team leaders accepted their oversight in this area and began to acknowledge the many and varied contributions their employees were making. The result was a significant and measurable improvement in moral.

Goals

Point marking end of race, object of effort or ambition destination, an aim or objective.

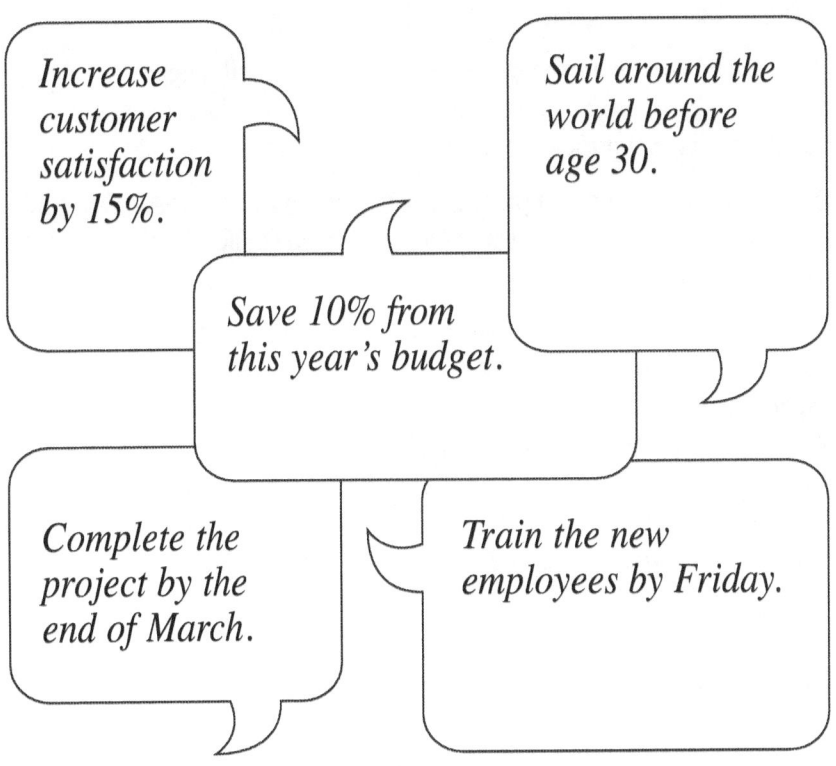

Increase customer satisfaction by 15%.

Sail around the world before age 30.

Save 10% from this year's budget.

Complete the project by the end of March.

Train the new employees by Friday.

Getting people to set goals can often be like pulling teeth. Imagine competing in a race without knowing where, or even if, there's a finish line? If you were asked to work on a car but it didn't matter if is ran or not, would you be enthusiastic? Would you put a lot of effort into a project when nobody seems to care if it's done or not?

Everyone knows about goals – often they are the New Year's resolutions people make at one time or another in their life. Goals are the plans to do something special, a dream to achieve, habits to eliminate or a career to advance. Fresh new goals, and a renewed commitment to purpose, are often the response to life-altering situations and events.

Goals give people something to look towards *as they deal with the day to day stuff of life.*

Sometimes high-value goals can feel overwhelming, unattainable, and distant and as such, are often forgotten or lose momentum over time. In this world of quick fixes, people want instant gratification. Yet instant gratification **is** achievable even with long-term goals.

When faced with goals that are HUGE, people can still engage in activities which, when done one at a time, accumulate and over time help them make significant progress to achieving their long-held dreams.

A climber I knew, who had made it to the summit of Everest, often told people that getting there was a matter of one slow, and often, labored, step at a time!

As a leader you'll want to support, encourage, and maybe even push your employees to set new goals, to stretch beyond their current capabilities, to reach higher levels, to develop their knowledge and skills, to expand their abilities by taking on new or expanded tasks. Occasionally people will cling tenaciously to their present role, the existing standards, and the current deliverables, overwhelmed by what would be involved in stepping out of their comfort zone.

On the other hand, some people set goals for themselves, optimistic and excited about stretching themselves, only to pull back later when the reality of what they have initiated, and the work involved sinks in. So finding a way to explore alternative approaches to make the goal a reality must be explored.

Lucas, a ten-year-old boy keen to fill his days when school was out, came to give me a hand in my garden. He and I had a plan, to collect as many leaves as we could to mulch my flower beds. I didn't have many deciduous trees so the plan entailed collecting them from the garden of an elderly lady who lived nearby. Together we raked and bagged leaves and mulched the beds. At the end of the day I mentioned I needed about 10 more bags to finish the job. Lucas said, "I'll get them from my neighbor." It was agreed I'd pay him the princely sum of $1 a bag! Excited about the promised $10 he set off home. Later he called me very excited. He's asked his neighbor if he could have her leaves and she'd paid him to take them away. So with the promise of doubling his money he'd set to work and filled the bags in record time. So goals may not be huge but they have to be important to the person who is accountable for executing the work.

In other instances the goals are dictated by the organization:

- **Establish a marketing plan for our new product.**
- **Develop an interactive web site for kids.**
- **Produce the photo journal for the annual report by August 1.**

As a leader you have the opportunity to provide a fresh perspective, to help employees see where gains can be made and still "stay the course."

Effective leaders position themselves as coaches; they take the time to examine the goals their employees have set, or need to meet, and help them identify the multitude of ways that progress may be made. Momentum builds momentum, so taking a few strides forward helps to build energy and enthusiasm.

Most of the major goals that overwhelm people include a myriad of small tasks, including phone calls to make, forms to complete, people to meet, things to research, areas to explore, skills to master and so on. By looking closely, individuals can begin to break down the goal into manageable "bite-sized chunks" and then proceed to take the many small steps that will ultimately help them reach their targets.

The individuals who set what many others would call "extreme" goals usually have a team in place to support their cause, desire or vision. The solo sail around the world, the climb to the top of Everest, the hot-air balloon trip across the Atlantic, are not single endeavors after all, but personal goals, supported from behind the scenes. The star performers nearly always have people who helped them take the steps necessary to reach their dream.

As an effective leader you can help your employees become star performers in your organization. Your support might take the form of listening to them talk through their plans; you may be called upon to cajole them, to provide some guidance, or discuss ways to mitigate problems.

One thing is certain, effective leaders find out what dreams, passions and goals lie in the minds of their employees – they take an interest, they ask if the employee wants support and what that support would look like – and they assist them in moving forward so they accomplish what they desire.

"I'd like to thank the people who helped me reach this goal today."

"If it hadn't been for… I would not be standing before you all now."

"I might be the one on the stage, accepting this trophy, but there was a whole team of people who helped me make this dream a reality."

A story about Goals

Westjet, a small independent airline launched itself onto the competitive field with a brand that differentiated it from the others. It was a no-frills, fun-filled flying experience like no other. At a time when the entire airline industry in North America was suffering huge losses it was an unusual time to be starting into a field saturated with well-established competitors, yet this airline knew it had something unique to offer.

This airline knew what it could do. It developed very clear goals and was determined to show the flying public that air travel didn't have to be a boring, hum-drum situation; it could liven things up and provide quality service at the same time.

- **Make it fun**
- **Fill a select market**
- **Cut the frills**

In no time, it showed their customers that the airline industry could deliver something to make its customers talk – and talk they did.

It **was** fun, it saved the customer's money, it flew where others did not, and it was a new brand of flying where everyone in the organization was clear about fulfilling its goals.

First-time passengers were entertained by a hip, young, fresh-faced flight crew who took the customary formal announcements to a new level. The familiar drone of announcements disappeared, replaced with light, off the cuff commentary. The content was there, its compliance with airline standards were upheld, yet the message was presented in a way that made the passengers sit up and take notice.

In time this "new kid on the block airline" was an attractive alternative to the familiar, well-established airline providers and in a time of bankruptcies a new airline was born.

Why were they successful right from the start? The leaders set goals. They stamped out a brand to make themselves different and they diligently and consistently "sold" those goals to every single one of their employees. Each employee knew, without a doubt, exactly how to behave so that they reflected the goals of their employer.

ABC
DEFG
HIJK
LMNO
PQRS
TUVW
XYZ

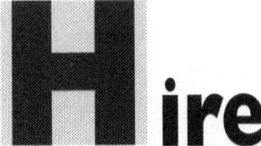

Hire

Payment by contract for use of thing or for personal service. Employ for wages. To obtain the use of someone for an agreed payment.

Thank you for bringing us your skills.

What special abilities can you offer our clients?

Welcome to our organization.

I'd like you all to meet...

We are fortunate to have retained you to work for us.

How can you find and retain great people? When leaders are faced with a staffing shortage there are many options available before following familiar methods for finding and retaining highly skilled and experienced employees. The traditional newspaper advertisement, the professional association's newsletter, the union hall, the various employment agencies are all samples of familiar places people turn to when looking to add or replace an employee.

Yet more and more companies are moving away from the newspaper advertisement which, often as not, results in hundreds of resumes to be read, screened and short-listed before the rounds of interviews begin. Many leaders look inside their organization and consider career development possibilities for employees. If they look ahead and consider succession planning they may find their current needs can be met within their existing workforce.

Finding the "right" person requires a great deal of thought. Long before thinking seriously about hiring someone, leaders usually engage in some pre-work. First of all they ask questions that might well save them from an expensive and time-consuming process.

- **Does this position really need to be filled?**
- **Does it need to be filled right now?**
- **Is this new position essential for the business to succeed?**
- **Does this position need to be full time, part time, temporary or seasonal, or could a job share situation suffice?**
- **Do I have an employee who might be ready for a career move into this area?**
- **Is there someone from within the current pool of employees who has indicated an interest in this work?**
- **Could the position be filled with someone less skilled, thereby creating a developmental opportunity?**
- **Can another employee be reasonably expected to train a new employee given the current workload?**
- **Can the workload be adjusted downwards temporarily without having a negative impact on others?**
- **If I was creating this department from scratch would I need this work to be done?**
- **What will happen if I don't fill the position?**

- **Is this a good time to take stock of what services we've been providing and the processes we have been following?**

As you can see from these questions, the effective leader stops long enough to ponder and consider these options. Only after a complete analysis of the situation can any decision be made to either fill or create a new position.

The work, and the climate in which people perform, are equally important. More and more leaders take stock of the current employee mix and strive to add people who will contribute to a harmonious working environment.

- **Who are the key players?**
- **What are the strengths and abilities of the current mix?**
- **What skills or talents would be valuable to add?**
- **What is the culture of the existing group?**
- **What is the working climate exhibited by the team?**
- **What would the existing team want in a new co-worker?**
- **What competencies are important for a new person to bring?**
- **How long have the present people been working together?**
- **Have there been any changes in positions, roles and responsibilities so that the working environment is dynamic, not static?**
- **Have the employees been cross-trained so that they can cover for each other or simply add some variety into the work?**

The effective leader knows they have to consider the existing team. A look at the current dynamics, the atmosphere and the culture will tell a lot about what type of person is most likely to fit in and be successful. All of these considerations must be weighed before any decision is made to hire someone or not.

Beyond these areas of consideration, the actual work must be assessed and a list of competencies needs to be compiled, which will form the foundation for any selection process.

- **What daily activities will this person assume?**
- **What activities are performed less frequently but are still highly important to the overall success of the position?**
- **What key knowledge or highly developed skills are required for each of the tasks associated with this position?**

- **What additional activities can you anticipate that this person will be required to perform six months to a year from now?**
- **What aptitude will be important for the future expanded role?**
- **What, if any, professional designation is required to fulfill the work?**

From an analysis of these answers and more the leader will be in a better position to either justify replacing an employee or adding a new person to the group. In addition, the leader will have a list of the essential knowledge or skills the person must either bring to the job or be prepared to develop fairly quickly.

Only when these steps have been completed can the leader proceed to source the right person.

The leader's own network often leads to recommendations regarding people, skills and special expertise which colleagues can then utilize. The casual conversation over lunch or on the golf course may lead to a name where a special service can be obtained. Key positions are found in the same manner.

The people you know and the relationships you form will be of paramount importance when you are seeking special skills and abilities to round out your current team.

The leader who wants to go through the hiring process smoothly and quickly will be well advised to work with their Human Resources department or a reliable, well-recognized recruitment agency to ensure the knowledge, skills and past work history of potential candidates are revealed. Nothing will de-rail team effectiveness more than a poorly matched employee who has managed to hide unpleasant and negative work habits only to have them re-surface in your organization.

The diligence undertaken at this stage will reward the leader, team members and the organization for years to come when the right person is offered the position and agrees to join your business. Knowing exactly what you are looking for in a new employee will mean you can carefully answer the applicant's questions about the new position and the responsibilities that accompany the role. It will mean you are not side-tracked by other appealing attributes the candidate brings forward, when in reality, you will not be in a position to use those skills and abilities in the role you are hoping to fill.

To hire someone because of what they offer, instead of staying focused on making a match between your needs and the candidate's abilities, will only lead to frustration on the part of the new employee who may well have thought that there were going to be more opportunities just around the corner. So completing a thorough needs analysis and developing a list of competencies will form the framework for the screening, interviewing and reference-checking steps that will help you find and retain the right person.

A story about Hiring

A manager in a medium sized organization was looking for a professional with a degree in forestry to manage some large-scale projects for a major client. The manager knew this person would be working with a team of technicians and that as the person had acquired a degree in forestry, in a specialty he required, he would be the ideal person to lead the project. Unfortunately this new employee's "people" skills were severely lacking even though he was a superbly qualified and experienced forester.

This manager realized too late that he had not considered the full range of services this person was going to be called upon to provide. The focus had been entirely devoted to the technical aspect of the job with little or no thought given to the relationships that needed to be forged and the team building aspects of the work.

This oversight occurred primarily because the manager was a "natural" at working with people and so assumed everyone could handle the complexities of working with others. It soon became clear that the professional forester's working style was creating problems between the team and the client, neither of which was readily corrected. Clearly some changes were required.

After conducting a more thorough assessment of the situation the forester was assigned to work on some highly technical aspects of the project where he could work alone and do his research and one of the technicians assumed the role of project leader, responsible for synergy with the team. The result was a more cohesive team able to manage the various stages of the project with ease.

Some early thought and analysis into the actual responsibilities for the project leader would have surfaced the possibility of the technician's interest in a new responsibility and would have led to a more focused interview with the forester.

In addition, by proceeding as they had, the forester was put into a position where he was "out of his depth" and experienced failure instead of success. Clearly, the up-front-time, to think things through can pay huge dividends for all of the parties involved.

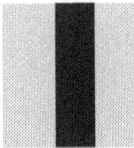 **nvolve**

To include, concern, entangle.

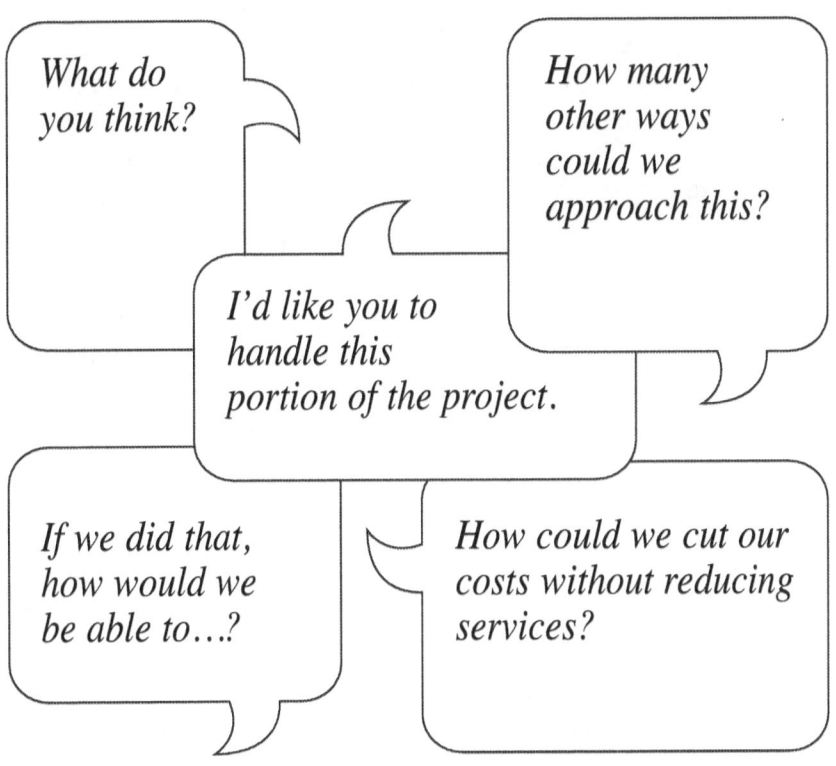

What do you think?

How many other ways could we approach this?

I'd like you to handle this portion of the project.

If we did that, how would we be able to…?

How could we cut our costs without reducing services?

Involving others is what some people do instinctively. Every strong leader knows that to accomplish great things it's best to reach out to great minds – often the ones right under their noses, their own employees. The people engaged in the daily routine of the work are often best positioned to identify opportunities where a procedure could be changed. They frequently know of better ways to serve a client, can pinpoint a strategy to save money, or single out places where a new product could be added.

So what's involved in involving others? Sometimes it's as simple as asking a question. In seeking information from others, leaders show they believe in them and their ideas; asking for input says I value you and your perspective. If you ask individuals for their opinion you'll find you end up with only a small handful of ideas. So, where do the really great ideas stem from, the ones that propel organizations forward and create sustained momentum?

Most effective leaders, who have made significant progress and breakthroughs into new business approaches, have employed group brainstorming sessions, customer focus groups or long-range strategic planning meetings. These group sessions have proven their worth in numerous organizations, whether it is a handful of key employees, some regular suppliers or long-standing clients; the collective brainpower produces astonishing results.

Yet to be effective each session must have the right mix of players, be well managed, follow clearly established boundaries and be led by someone who can ensure there is open, frank communication with structure and a record-keeping process. In other words, a great professional facilitator. The leader may not be the best person to facilitate this process as they often have too much at stake and can inadvertently steer the conversation along paths which are not productive. On top of that they have a history with each of the participants and unless they can put that aside and remain completely open to whatever surfaces, they may be frustrated with the outcome. A skilled facilitator will be able to handle all of the dynamics that occur during group sessions.

A framework is essential and has to be established up front to keep people focused on the results and the purpose of the gathering. The leader or facilitator will apply their knowledge of group dynamics knowing that even though the session may appear "free and open"' they have to maintain some control over the process.

Many of these leaders or facilitators will prepare people in advance of the meeting. They explain the purpose of the meeting and what they want to accomplish by the end of the time together. This enables the participants to give some thought to the topic and come prepared to engage in the process and contribute their ideas.

Effective leaders know that the combined input from a group of people almost always generates the most compelling ideas. They know that by relinquishing some of the decision-making to the group, everyone wins; employees, clients, suppliers, shareholders or taxpayers.

Involving others, however, does not mean you, as leader, give up the right to make the final decision or manage your business. As a leader you are frequently expected and need to decide on a variety of business issues. However, the decisions made by leaders who have engaged others are generally more solid, well thought out and stand the test of time, as a result of input, ideas and suggestions from these participants.

As a result of seeking input, leaders have

- **gained insight into new products their clients are seeking**
- **streamlined processes that save the budget significantly**
- **made production adjustments that have dramatically improved safety**
- **established new marketing strategies that have reached many new clients,** and
- **formed joint ventures which have benefited hundreds of employees and their customers.**

To become an "involving" leader you need to think carefully about the things you are willing to open up for discussion. Asking a group of customers a wide-open question about which products they want you to carry, will lead to a huge broad-based list of items that you may not be able to sort through. Conversely, asking your customers to identify which brands of ice cream they want you to carry, and any particular flavors they want, will greatly assist you in offering products they want and minimize the old stock from your freezers.

While these may seem like simple examples of involving others they can make an enormous and positive impact on the participants. In most cases, they very quickly see the results of their input, leading them to offer more ideas, readily and frequently.

But involvement doesn't just stop at asking for input and ideas. Involving others means letting them join with others, maybe even the leader, by handling aspects of special projects. It's about sharing the work and giving people opportunities to make a new, interesting and different contribution. Perhaps there's a new initiative that has been discussed and accepted that the employees can take through to full implementation. If it's something the employee is interested in they may welcome the opportunity to make a contribution that uses new skills or knowledge. If the employees are charged with enacting the steps they identified, it truly becomes "their baby" so to speak.

A word of caution! Proceed carefully. Involvement will be eroded very quickly when there's an absence of visible results. People want, in fact need to see the results of their input.

If there's any doubt about what can or cannot be changed, do not ask for input!

Wait until you are sure you can proceed with at least some aspect of the topic or the interest and enthusiasm you generate will be dampened, maybe for good when nothing comes of their work.

A story about Involving

A small-scale organic farmer, who was struggling to make a living, arranged a meeting between some restaurant owners and other organic farmers to see if there was a way in which the farmers could supply fresh organic produce to restaurants.

The restaurant owners wanted a reliable supply of locally grown fruits, vegetables, eggs and chickens so they could advertise that they used "fresh local organic ingredients." Unfortunately they had been unable to find any farmer with the ability to supply all of their needs on a sustained basis.

The restaurants didn't want to deal with a stream of farmers and the farmers didn't want to have to go to many different restaurants all over town.

At the meeting the farmers and chefs talked about the dilemma and finally reached a solution. A group of seven high-end restaurants contracted with one experienced farmer, who became the coordinator. She in turn contracted with several other organic farmers in the area. The chefs developed a list of produce that they wanted the coordinator to provide on a daily, weekly and seasonal basis and she then arranged with the farmers to grow exactly what the restaurants needed. A daily pick-up and delivery system was established which freed, the farmers from making their own deliveries. Now they could direct all of their energy on growing, harvesting and packing a few products which they knew were going to be bought.

The result of this endeavor was a stable supply of organic ingredients for the restaurants who finally felt confident going ahead with the advertising program. This arrangement also created a reliable income for the farmers who now only planted and grew what they knew they would sell.

The patrons of these restaurants came to know they could depend on organic ingredients in their meals and felt good that these restaurants were supporting local farmers.

A B C
D E F G
H I J K
L M N O
P Q R S
T U V W
X Y Z

Justice

Equitable, fair, deserved, well-founded, proper, appropriate, behavior to another, which is strictly in accord with currently, accepted ethical law.

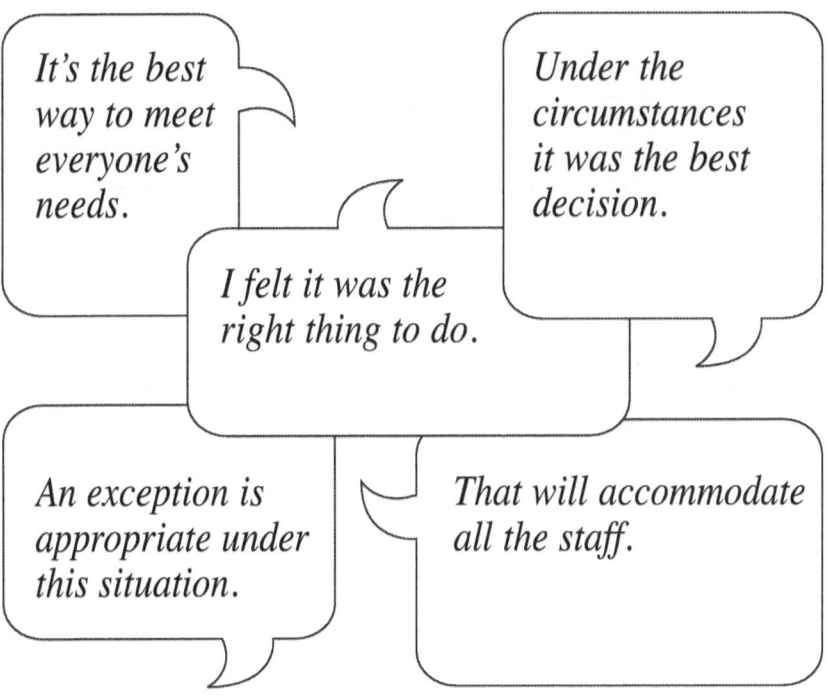

It's the best way to meet everyone's needs.

Under the circumstances it was the best decision.

I felt it was the right thing to do.

An exception is appropriate under this situation.

That will accommodate all the staff.

Justice reaches far beyond our legal system. Employees want their leaders to be fair and just. Yet in order to be fair, leaders often have to make decisions that may appear unfair. This occurs when they do not seem to be treating everyone equally. But fair and just is NOT the same as equal. Justice is about using available information, considering the person's needs, examining the circumstance and the options available so as to make the best possible decision.

The employee who is going to be away from work for a few weeks, undergoing surgery wants the leader to recognize the present situation and then make allowances to fit the current need. The decision to bring in a temporary employee on a short-term basis to cover the surgery-bound employee's job may well be a just and reasonable step in this circumstance. Or the leader may decide that another employee who has shown an interest in the job, may well benefit from a short period in the role, and this is the just and reasonable thing to do.

Is it fair that the other employees have to pick up some of the slack while their colleague is off? Certainly. And most employees would understand their leader's decisions as being just and fair. They would probably expect, and rightly so, that under the same circumstances they would be treated in the same way.

Justice really comes into question when identical or similar situations present themselves and the leader handles each one in a very different manner. For example, if two employees are unable to complete assignments on time due to other pressures and one employee is given an extra week to get it done while the other is chastised for failing to meet the deadline, there would, in all likelihood, be some grumbling about the lack of justice.

Whenever there is the perception of favoritism you can expect grumbling, discontent and a questioning of the leader's integrity. Once a belief is established, people generally look for evidence to prove their position or belief. This means that every act or decision by the leader would be scrutinized and evaluated by the employee, particularly if the employee feels the injustice has been directed at him or her.

This is most evident when there are close links between employees. A husband and wife in the same company, a son and daughter in the same organization, the cousin, nephew, uncle, or any manner of close relationships can be cause for extra scrutiny. When a decision is made that affects an employee there will always be individuals who, if they don't like the choice, will question the leader's decision. They will say to themselves, "it's because it's her own son that he got that job", or "we all know they are buddies that's why they are allowed to work on the same shift", or "she got away with being late because her husband is the shop steward" or "the promotion was given to her because she's the manager's niece.

Conversely, the leader must make sure that "just" decisions are made *even though there are strong bonds between employees*. Denying an employee a promotion "because it might be interpreted as favoritism" is unjust and unwarranted. Not allowing close family members to work on the same shift when it's clearly to their advantage to travel together because someone might think you have "created a special deal for them" is unjust.

In these situations, when there is the potential for misinterpretation, it is even more important for the leader to examine the decision-making thoughts and patterns. Has the leader been "just" in the way the decision was handled? Has the leader made sure all employees involved understand the rationale used to make what was deemed to be a "just" and reasonable approach? In times like this, the leader must make his or her decision transparent – and there will still be doubts in some employee's minds.

The wise leader makes sure that employees are treated in as "just" a manner as possible and that they know each decision was made after considering the situation carefully. The wise leader also makes his or her rationale for the decisions known to all and any parties.

A story about Justice

A manager of a very popular restaurant in a tourist center developed a unique way of serving his patrons. He hired waiters, waitresses and bus boys based on their interest in teamwork. This was not a restaurant where the servers had their own set tables to care for. In this restaurant any and all servers were expected to take care of any and all guests. For example, if a plate of food came from the kitchen, the first person to walk past the food would take it to the guest, regardless of where they were located in the restaurant – everyone took care of everyone.

In traditional restaurants, most waiters, waitresses and bus boys are acknowledged for their service by receiving tips from patrons based on how well they have taken care of the guests. So how could the waiters and waitresses receive the financial acknowledgement when there was no one clear individual to acknowledge?

The manager created a recognition and feedback box with paper and envelopes for the guests to use. Each table had pens and paper and patrons were encouraged to jot down their comments. From the person's name that they wanted to acknowledge or a special service someone had given, to the quality of the food or the décor, all were open for comment. The envelopes could be deposited in a box beside the door along with any financial contribution the guest felt was appropriate.

The manager said too often the waiters and waitresses are the only ones to hear feedback and receive tips but it takes a whole team to run a fine dining establishment, and that extends far beyond the walls of the restaurant.

"Our customers tell us how they enjoy the special delicacies our chef's prepare from local ingredients and we can then pass that on to the farmer. We hear about the cutlery and napkins, the lighting and the flowers, as well as the seating and the spacing and this feedback helps us to be even more effective. In addition our employees are rewarded handsomely for their work as most of our patrons provide a healthy tip along with their comments as they are only too glad to have this opportunity to say their piece." The manager told me the financial bonus is distributed equally amongst all of the staff – from the hostess to those behind the scenes doing the dishes – in recognition of the team effort it takes to make the whole restaurant be successful.

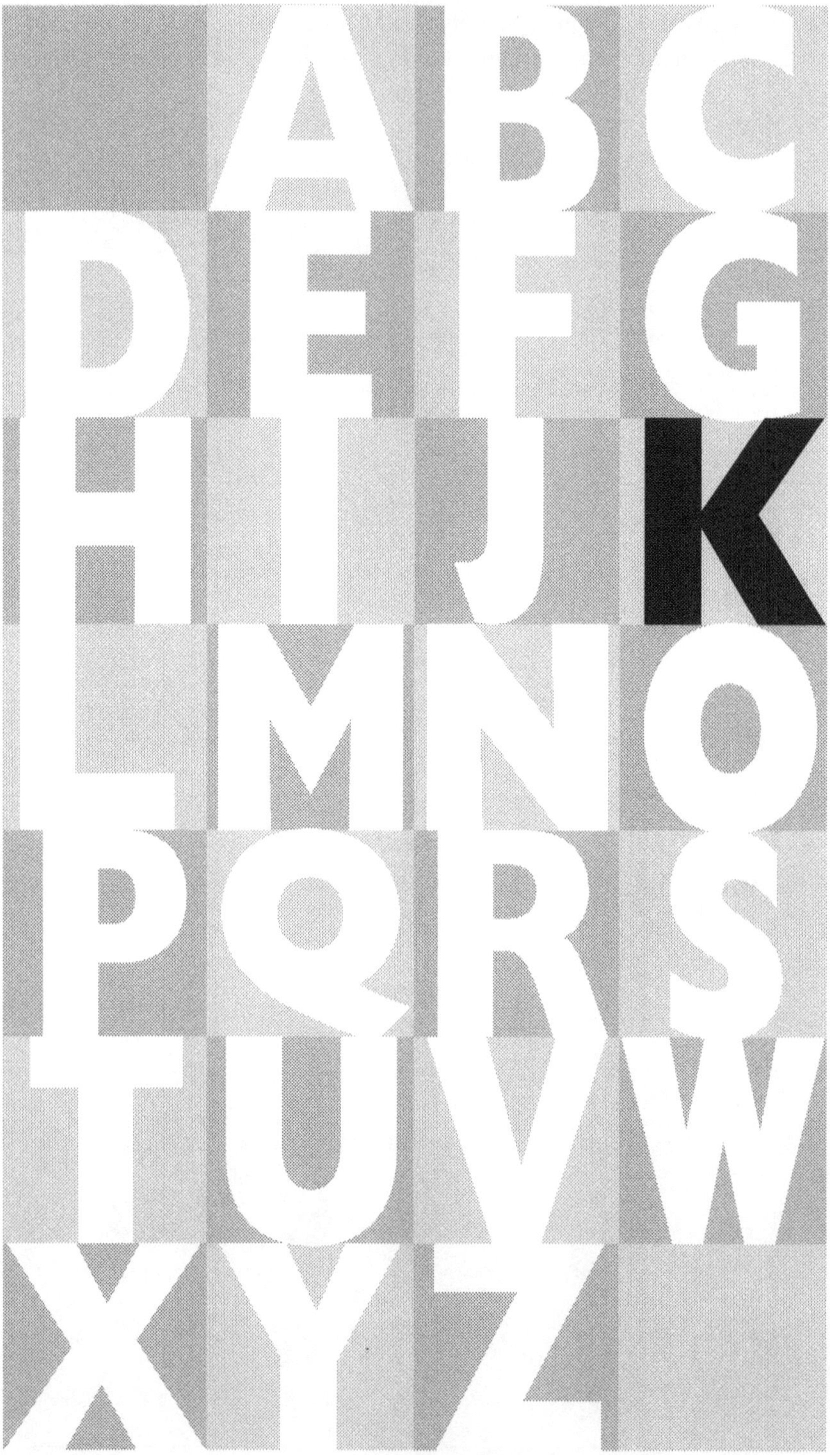

ABC
DEFG
HIJK
LMNO
PQRS
TUVW
XYZ

Knowledge

To be acquainted with by experience, to be in possession of facts, to be informed, to recognize, have personal experience of.

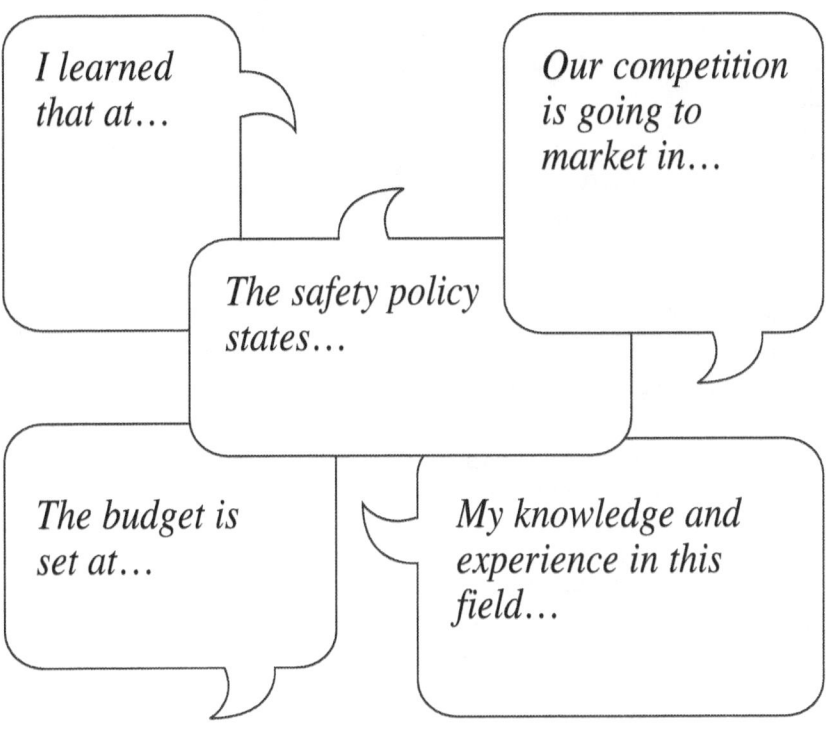

I learned that at…

Our competition is going to market in…

The safety policy states…

The budget is set at…

My knowledge and experience in this field…

K nowledge is power. You've heard it before but it's worth repeating and remembering. The people who can present an idea followed by solid, up-to-date details, or can defend their point of view with facts and data, can influence others more readily than those who strive to make an impact without such information.

How the knowledge is attained is more important in some organizations than in others. Sometimes job postings will specify a desire for a combination of education and/or experience, meaning in their eyes that they count for the same in the organization's mind.

In other instances the appropriate credentials from a recognized institution is the *only* acceptable form of knowledge and education that will be considered. Knowledge is not the same as skill. Skill is acquired by the application of knowledge and through adjustment, frequency and exposure over time.

People can't provide quality service, whatever their position, without adequate knowledge about the work being done. Leaders either hire knowledgeable employees who bring their expertise and experience to the workplace or they have to provide the training and hands-on opportunities that will enable the employee to perform to the required standards.

Knowledge must be gained somewhere if people are to be deemed competent and capable to fulfill the requirements of their position to a high or professional standard.

As a leader your own knowledge will often be put to the test when employees turn to you for guidance and direction. Effective leaders make sure they keep up-to-date on the latest leadership thinking, technological advances or strategies that will build and strengthen their business. In addition, effective leaders surround themselves with competent and knowledgeable staff; often better educated than the leader, who together form a strong team, with each person able to make a valuable contribution.

This does not mean you, as a leader, have to have the answers in your head. A library of current materials is a perfectly acceptable resource to be referred to when the exact problem requires more detail than can be stored and remembered with ease. A copy of the collective agreement is a case in point. The Workers' Compensation Board regulations are an example of a detailed document with numerous clauses and sub-clauses making it onerous to remember every detail. Some facts need to be retrieved on an "as and when required" basis and will allow the employee to move forward to complete some aspect of the job with greater confidence.

How leaders gain knowledge is as varied as leadership styles. For some, the knowledge will be gained through networking with peers in their particular trade or profession, participating in conferences, by doing some research, making presentations to special interest groups, reading, attending workshops or contracting with a coach or mentor.

Knowledge on its own is of little value however, unless there are avenues for the knowledge to be applied. Knowing the steps involved in changing a flat tire won't help you on a dark winter night if you've never had the opportunity to try your hand at actually following the steps and completing the task.

Knowing is not enough. Knowing is not the goal. The application of knowledge is essential for true learning to take place and that application must be on-going or the knowledge that becomes second nature, or the skills to execute some function in a smooth and easy manner, will become stale and ineffective.

This learning and seeking knowledge is what permeates the halls, lunchrooms and offices of learning organizations, places where everyone constantly strives to examine what is working or not. In these organizations you'll find a lot of debriefing, post-project analysis, and post mortems. These employees are striving to find alternatives, to examine habits and patterns that no longer serve their best interests or help them meet the goals of the organization. They discuss, explore, examine and look with a critical eye at everything, with the objective of making things better. The employees who seek to learn want to make things more efficient, more effective, more fun, more productive and more satisfying.

The learning organization never rests on its laurels; it's constantly evolving, changing, adapting, modifying, streamlining, and trying new approaches. For some, the constant state of flux is painful, and they agonize over the loss of status quo, while for others it's thrilling and exciting to see new products come to market, new customers line up to use their services, or new ways to work together. One thing is certain, it's never dull.

The effective leader ensures that their employees are provided with any information that they have personally acquired, information that is not confidential, that will enable these employees to be more effective. They want a team that is up-to-date with emerging trends and recent thinking.

Knowledge must be passed on, discussed, explored and tested in order for individuals and organizations to thrive and flourish.

The leader who is committed to others' growth and development is a constant source of information. They check others' understanding and find ways to close gaps in their knowledge. They seek opportunities for others to learn and become skillful. This diligent pursuit of information can be contagious. Employees often find the increased information energizing; it gives them additional confidence in doing their job, and allows for better decision-making and more empowerment.

The organization built on the pursuit of knowledge thrives. The employees reap the rewards from being part of an organization that is dedicated to continuous learning.

A story about Knowledge

A television commercial for Thrifty Foods a thriving and rapidly growing chain of grocery stores in western Canada, shows a new employee being put through a series of questions. *"Where would you find…? How do you prepare…? Which aisle is… in? What's the price of… today? What's this?"* And so on.

The employee is shown rapid-firing answers and showing customers to the products throughout the store. The commercial ends with. "Okay! You're ready to go to work, to give our customers what they have come to expect from all of our employees." This commercial is based on true-to-life situations you can find in any one of their locations.

Customers in these stores can go to anyone, that's right "anyone" and ask for help finding a product and you won't find them saying "that's not my department." Not only that, but the employee will escort you to the aisle and point out the product you were asking for – plus some alternatives or specials which you might not have known about.

Each and every employee is given the knowledge to help each and every customer. In addition, you'll find incredibly well informed employees who are "department specialists". I overheard a young man explaining the difference between Japanese and Chinese tangerines to one customer and then showed her how one peeled easier and was ideal for children's lunches. Another day I heard an employee explaining his favourite way to prepare halibut as he was wrapping it up for a customer, while yet another listed the ingredients in a cheesecake for a customer with a dietary concern.

The knowledge each of these employees had gained during their training and on-the-job coaching allowed them to provide exemplary service, which far exceeded most customers' expectations. It gave them pride in their work as evidenced by the smiles on their faces as customer after customer thanked them for the service-plus treatment.

These employees have helped to earn the company a loyal and growing following. When you ask a customer, as they enter or leave, why they shop in this particular store, you're likely to hear "it's the service and attention I get from the staff." The dedication to educating and making their employees as knowledgeable as possible is paying off as more and more stores open up in small and large communities all across the west, each one with its own brand of excellence.

ABCDEFGHIJKLMNOPQRSTUVWXYZ

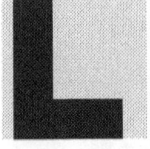 # Listening

To use one's ears consciously in order to hear, to pay attention, to be influenced by, make effort to hear something, hear person speaking with attention.

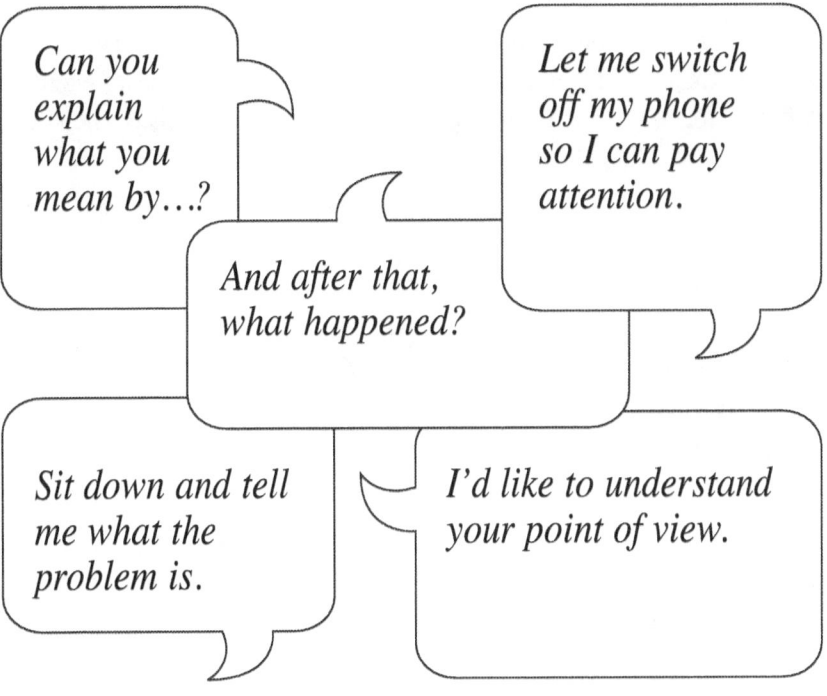

Can you explain what you mean by…?

Let me switch off my phone so I can pay attention.

And after that, what happened?

Sit down and tell me what the problem is.

I'd like to understand your point of view.

L istening is a long-neglected skill. Have you ever had the experience of being truly listened to? Do you recall the satisfaction you felt from being heard, from someone giving you their undivided attention? Do you remember the pleasure you felt from knowing someone cared enough to pay close attention?

Not many people can say that they experience true listening on a regular basis. Most people can recall one or maybe two occasions when they had someone truly give them their undivided attention and the impact of that deep and conscious listening has stood out in their mind. It's sad to think that such a small thing, one that can make such a huge difference to people, is so seldom done or done well. At work, listening is key to working well with others. If your instructions are not heard, or the listener was distracted, then all manner of things can occur that were unintended.

Listening is not hearing! Hearing is a passive act, which only requires fully functioning ears. Hearing occurs even while we are asleep as ears are permanently open unlike eyes and mouths.

Listening, on the other hand, requires effort, concentration and a willingness to shut out potentially distracting sounds as much as possible. Listening is the ultimate sign of respect since it shows interest in the person and their message and helps to build confidence when the speaker notices that someone is really paying attention.

The leader who believes in and wants to develop strong listening skills needs to understand the operation of a brain being subjected to the input of data. Consider the following information.

Research shows that the brain is capable of taking in verbal information at about 500 words per minute, while the average speaker talks at about 125 words per minute. So clearly, there is "brain time" to spare while receiving verbal messages and this "spare time" is put to use in a variety of ways.

The listener is making conscious and unconscious judgments and assessments about the person who is providing the information. In addition they are dealing simultaneously with their own "internal thoughts" which may or may not have anything to do with the speaker.

Research shows that some fairly common thoughts related to the speaker may reveal unconscious biases. The person may be young, *too young* in the listener's mind to know about the topic in depth, or, conversely, **has the latest information** as they're fresh out of university. The person may be elderly and this could lead to thoughts regarding their knowledge of the subject, such as **are they experienced** or **out-of-date?**

If an individual is surprised to find someone in a non-traditional role, for example a female electrician who arrives at a residence, or an office receptionist who is male, it's quite common to find, however fleetingly, that people question their suitability for the role, and even their ability to professionally do the job.

Clothing will also have an impact on the listener's ability to "hear" the message. What expectations are supported or violated? Is this way of dressing appropriate in the listener's mind? What do the bright red fingernails say to the listener, what messages do the unpolished shoes tell the listener. How about the fine leather briefcase, or the expensive watch?

So the listener is supporting the verbal information with visual clues which may or may not be aligned with the content.

Now, let's examine the internal "brain noise" going on inside the listener's head that has nothing to do with the speaker or the verbal message being provided. Research shows that a continual barrage of thoughts race through our heads while we try to listen attentively. A look inside the listener's head might reveal these thoughts: *I must remember to call… I forgot to pick up the dry cleaning… I've got to finish the report after he/she leaves, when did… say they were going to call…and so on and so on.*

The effective leader, and committed listener, will make every effort to shut down their own internal "noise" and notice the biases that are creeping into their thoughts.

Challenging? You bet. Manageable? Yes, with time and with practice.

To truly listen you need to minimize distractions.

- **Have your calls held if you're in a meeting.**
- **Put down your pen.**

- **Push aside your paperwork.**
- **Face the person speaking.**
- **Maintain eye contact.**

Confirm you were listening and want to know more by paraphrasing – feeding back some content to let the speaker know you are following and want to understand. *"So you asked for the report to be ready by Monday."* *"Let me see, you say John is going to work on it with you is that right?"*

Add in empathizing and the demonstration of listening becomes even stronger. *"Yes, it's annoying when…."* *"I'd feel frustrated too if…."* *"It's worrying when…."*

Questions are also very powerful tools for showing you are listening. Have some "tell me more" questions ready.

- *What happened after that?*
- *Who else was involved?*
- *What did the customer say next?*
- *Where did this occur?*
- *When did you first notice?*

Demonstrate your interest in how the person feels about their information by matching their mood as much as possible. Be serious if they are serious, smile if they're relaxed, show concern if they are worried, laugh if they are funny. All of this shows the speaker you are paying attention.

The most effective leaders know that by giving their time and attention to others, by making it obvious they listen, they will build stronger relationships. By putting aside distractions, by feeding back some content, by asking for more information and matching the mood of the speaker, they build rapport, strengthen teamwork and foster strong ties.

A Story about Listening

A keynote speaker at a national conference I attended was described as a dynamic, professional and animated communicator who had worked in the US National Parks system for many years. He was scheduled to lead a one-hour keynote address on the role of the park ranger. Specifically, he'd talk about interacting with guests and how the ranger can build strong customer relations and repeat visits.

The time had come for his presentation and the auditorium was packed; not a seat was empty and some people even stood at the back. People were talking quietly, checking the stage, and a hush descended when a door opened and a man appeared. He walked to the microphone and before he'd even tapped it to say, *"Testing, testing"* the audience started to talk again. He wasn't the speaker after all. The man at the microphone wore grubby coveralls, had a woolen hat and big work boots. He was clearly here to set things up for the speaker.

But the man then fished in his pocket and drew out a few sheets of paper and placed them on the podium, smiled at the audience and stood waiting for us to become quiet. And we did. A hush descended slowly until a deadly silence permeated through the auditorium. Some people were seen exchanging looks of surprise that the keynote speaker, instead of being dressed in suit and tie looked like a technician from behind the scenes.

I remember my reaction – I examined my brochure to check if I was in the right place at the right time.

This "technician" and not the "polished and professional speaker" that I had been expecting, then commenced. He thanked the audience for coming to hear him speak, and as he did so his notes slipped from the podium. He stooped to retrieve them, tried to flatten them out, laughed a bit, put them back on the lectern and started again, back at the beginning, to thank the audience for coming.

He then tapped the mike again, "testing, testing, can you hear me alright?" A few people answered "yes" rather impatiently. A quiet, low murmur began to rise from around the auditorium as people exchanged startled looks and one person at the back got up to leave, clearly disappointed by what appeared to be a different presentation from what had been touted.

Then the speaker started to laugh. He yelled to the man at the back, *"wait, please don't go,"* and he stripped off the coveralls and revealed a suit. He removed the hat and slicked down his hair with a small comb, and pulled a tie from his pocket and put it on, tightened it in place and then paused, laughed and asked, *"Is that better?"* We all laughed in return and roared *"yes."* He then went on to talk in an animated and delightful manner about first impressions and how they can influence people's willingness to listen.

He asked the man who'd been about to leave if he'd decided, when he stood up to go, that he didn't want to listen to this unprofessional keynote speaker. The man laughed and replied, "you bet."

He then went on to use his little bit of fun with the audience to illustrate that, in general, we want people to "look the part." And he went on to say that whether we realize it or not, we have expectations of what is "proper and correct" in all manner of situations, that conflicting images will influence the willingness to listen. He certainly drove his message home with his one-minute example.

Meetings

A gathering, to come face to face, a coming together of people often for business purposes..

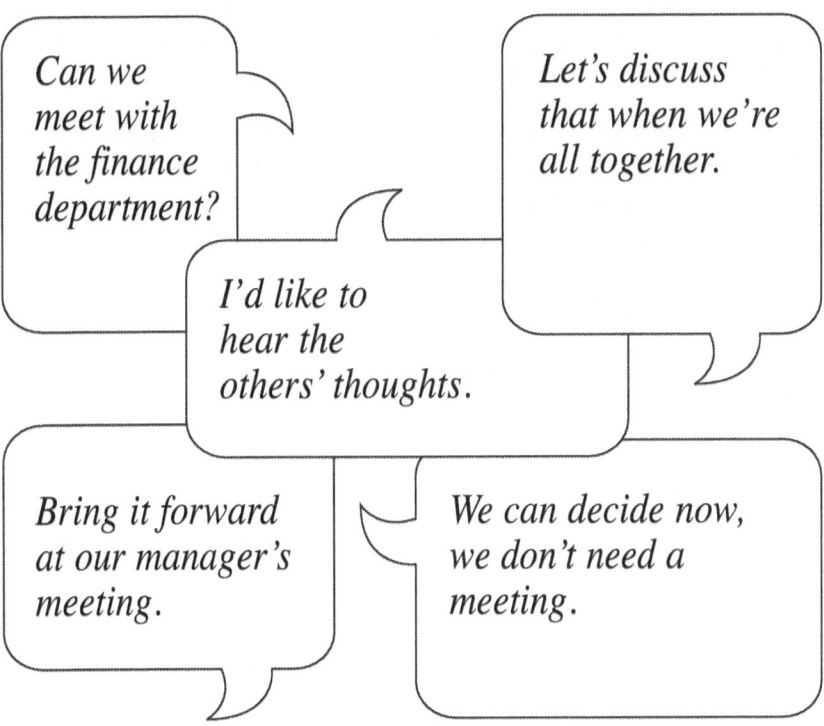

Can we meet with the finance department?

Let's discuss that when we're all together.

I'd like to hear the others' thoughts.

Bring it forward at our manager's meeting.

We can decide now, we don't need a meeting.

Meetings can be, and often are, the bane of a manager's life. Yet, when well planned and managed, they can be the most valuable part of the business world and are increasingly, the place where important decisions are crystallized.

The leader who wishes to become known for their skillful management of meetings, those attended by participants with diverse and perhaps controversial points of view, will need to develop some specialized skills in group facilitation. But, before looking at the actual meeting process, there are three other factors effective leaders must take into consideration.

- **First, the advance work to set up the meeting**
- **Secondly, the actual meeting process**
- **Finally, the follow up that ensures action plans unfold as orchestrated.**

All three of these parts require careful thought, as they are critical for meetings to be productive and valuable.

A workshop title "Why Intelligent People Make Bad Decisions" intrigued me and caused some pondering. I wondered, when people are gathered together in a meeting, why do they end up with poor decisions?

It seems that in order for meetings to be successful it's important to establish a framework, a structure that will more likely lead to better discussions and ultimately the best decisions.

The pre-meeting considerations must be examined long before any meeting is planned. First and foremost some thinking must take place around the need for the meeting.

- **Why do you want to have a meeting?**
- **Is it really essential?**
- **What do you want to accomplish?**
- **Who are the key people who must be there?**
- **What do you want them to think about prior to the meeting?**
- **What information needs to be distributed in advance?**

To start, consider the first point – why have a meeting? It's important to determine if getting people together is really the most effective use of everyone's time and, if the meeting will enable some result that would not otherwise be able to proceed.

Challenge traditional thinking and ask yourself, "is there another more effective way to handle this issue/topic/information?" In some instances, upon reflection, the leader will see that a simple memo, email, telephone call or five minutes at the end of another meeting will suffice.

Once it's been determined that a meeting IS important, the next important question to ask is, "what do I want to accomplish?" If you are going to walk out of the meeting feeling the time was well spent, what would you focus on, what decisions would be made and what actions plans would be established? Being clear about your intended outcome will greatly assist you in deciding who should be present and will aid you in facilitating the dialogue.

So once you've determined a meeting is the best approach and you're clear about what you want to accomplish, your next step is to determine who "needs" to be there. Filling the room and including everyone who thinks they should have been invited is **not** the way to proceed.

- **Who has the data, facts, information that will be required to make a decision?**
- **Who will be responsible for implementing the plan?**
- **Who will be affected in a significant way?** (When there are changes, everyone will be affected to some degree, but we're talking about a substantial impact here.)

So while it might be nice to pad the room with your supporters, this won't necessarily lead to a more productive and valuable meeting. Keep the numbers down to the few key players as this is much more likely to enable you to move ahead.

The final question before the meeting proceeds, is do these people need to attend for the whole meeting? Sometimes a person can join the others for a brief time to deal with some issue that requires their particular area of expertise, freeing them up to continue with other aspects of their work.

How many times have you sat through topics in meetings that have no impact on you and your team when your participation should have been reduced to an hour or less?

Make sure you consider the role each person is required to play and ask yourself if they need to sit through the entire meeting or can they just slip in for a portion of the time.

So effective leaders ask themselves some questions that will determine who should be present and how long these people need to attend.

- **Is financial input required?**
- **Who can give approvals?**
- **Will a person from the union be available to provide input?**
- **Perhaps someone from Human Resources is required to provide staffing input, or**
- **Will the legal department have something to say about a new approach you are considering?**

Consider this; not all of these people need to be at the meeting to have input. Perhaps their information can be obtained ahead of time so the facts and details are presented. If it's important to hear from an individual or to pose questions to someone, then consider asking the person to slip in for ten minutes or so, to address a key point. Do not tie them up unnecessarily.

Finally, the best-run meetings always have people who are well prepared. These participants have had access to and read information that was provided to them so they are prepared to discuss the subject. In other words the participants come ready to get to work. They know what the leader wants to accomplish and they come armed with the facts and resources to enable an in-depth and detailed discussion to occur.

So, after the decision has been made that a meeting is essential, the outcome has been established and the participants have been identified, then the leader must consider how best to manage the discussion. Once again some pre-thinking will serve the leader well.

- **What is known about the participants' viewpoint on the topic?**
- **Is this relatively simple or is it a highly controversial and complex issue?**
- **How much time will it take to get all of the facts on the table?**
- **How much time will be required to reach the goal?**

Once these areas have been addressed, group dynamics must be well thought out. Whenever a group of people come together to share opinions, provide their perspective and try to reach a decision, there are sure to be challenging exchanges. Some people are verbal and may even dominate the conversation, while others are reflective, pondering and considering information or ideas, and so are much quieter.

Some people will withhold information if they perceive it to be outside of the group's accepted direction for fear of adding conflict or delaying the meeting's end. On the other hand, others may well try to add new positions and strive to delay the decision making, hoping for any changes or actions that might emerge, to be delayed.

The wise leader knows that managing people and their input, while considering the direction the conversation will take, requires significant skill. Some leaders elicit the group's help in making the meeting productive, thereby making its success a joint responsibility.

Using an agenda, setting a framework, establishing boundaries and then applying a deep focused, listening, advocacy and enquiry model will make a much more productive meeting, leading to the best possible decision.

The leader who fosters an environment whereby everyone is respected – the vocal and the quiet, the timid and the self-confident, the challenger and the one who agrees – will often garner support due to the nature of the discussion. The effective facilitation of the meeting is a combination of skills, many of which are covered in this book

*(See **B**: – Boundaries, **C** – Communication, **Q** – Questioning,*
L *– Listening)*

Once a decision has been reached, actions must follow. These actions need to be owned and assumed by the participants. Commitments need to be made to the leader and the others who may well depend on a colleague to do their part before being able to add their own portion. So, determining "who" will do "what" and by "when" is the last step before adjourning the meeting.

Following the meeting, each participant should receive a copy of the group's decision, the actions, plans, and a list of the people responsible for the next steps. The leader, armed with these commitments, is better able to follow-up to ensure deadlines are met.

A story about Meetings

A large pulp mill was undergoing a major expansion and a large and diverse team of people would be required to orchestrate the construction and the multitude of decisions that would need to take place.

The chief engineer had planned a series of meetings and he called on my services as a professional facilitator. Many of the participants came from around the world so the international make-up of the group added language challenges to the mix. Staff from within the mill had their own agendas and the need to create structure yet allow discussions and decision-making to proceed could prove challenging. The preliminary meetings were intended to bring the entire project team together so they could meet.

The team included not only engineers from Canada, the US, Sweden and Germany but also equipment suppliers from Sweden and Finland, production personnel from their own mill, and maintenance employees, trainers, designers, electricians, pipe fitters, plumbers, and so on. It hadn't taken the chief engineer long to realize that facilitating a discussion amongst such a large and diverse team would require special skills. So he stood aside and let me take the lead.

Over the next five months the entire team of over 40 met once a month for a whole day, while small sub-groups met more often. The small groups often joined the full day sessions and everyone operated within clearly defined boundaries.

At the end of the project, when the mill was up and running, the chief engineer said, "This project moved ahead on time and under budget due in large part to the success of our meetings. Sound decisions were made because right at the beginning the facilitator made us listen to each other and she asked the questions we missed and kept us on track."

Nurturing

To provide for, to nourish. Fostering care, to provide those conditions which are favorable to healthy growth.

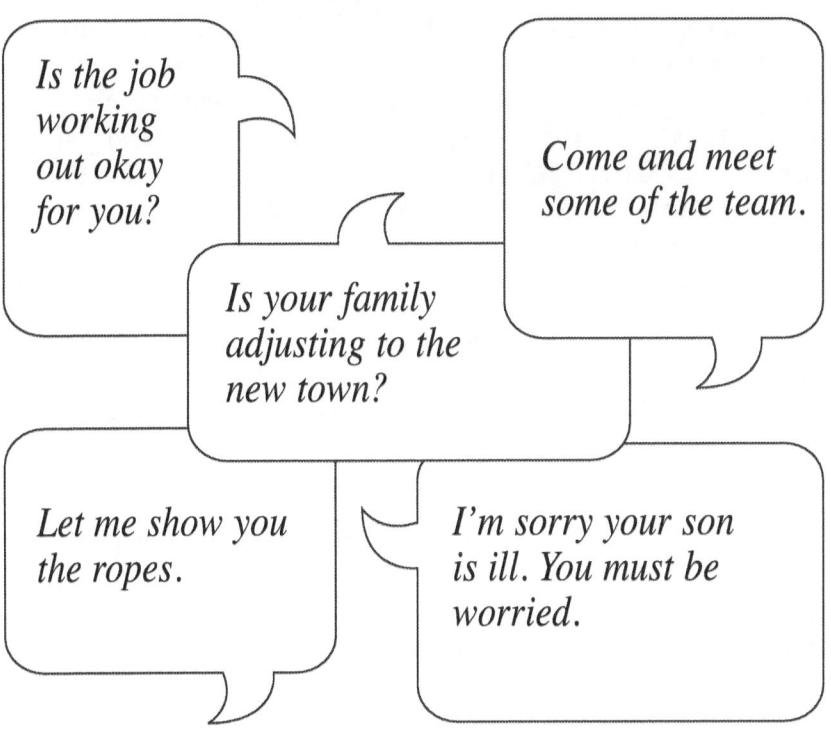

Not enough companies care about their people to the full extent possible. Great employers, on the other hand, truly care about their people and have people lining up to join their organizations. They make sure their working environment, policies, benefit packages, educational subsidies and parental leave or time to manage elderly parents are accommodated to the best of their ability. It's well known that research shows that to build a strong, cooperative and harmonious workplace the most effective leaders look beyond the work their employees are engaged in to the people and their lives in general. That does not mean they probe and pry into their personal affairs, but it does mean they take an interest in the things that are important in the employee's life.

In addition, they make the workplace as tension-free as possible, a place where people can contribute their best, knowing they are supported and encouraged to be themselves.

Frequently these places of employment have extra-curricular events and activities that employees are encouraged to attend. They may be small, casual, company-funded events to honor a birthday, a special milestone, an employee's new baby, a retirement or marriage. In some cases the time and funds will be provided through a social committee staffed by volunteers. Mid-summer BBQs, family picnics, baseball and golf tournaments and other special activities all contribute to the well being of the work unit. The time employees spend together at work and the demands for results, often limits the opportunities to really get to know each other as individuals.

The wise leader encourages and cultivates a climate whereby employees can relax and have a bit of fun *while they work*. Whether it's the joke of the day, the Friday jeans tradition, the doughnuts for all, or a competition to dress up for Halloween, it's the little things that really DO matter.

Asking the new employee about how the family is settling-in to the new town, enquiring if the children are enjoying their new school or giving the employee the name of a fitness center or tennis club, all help to make the new employee feel welcomed and cared for.

The new employee, particularly someone new to town, is often an easy and natural place to begin, but what about your long-term employees?

When did you last check on them and their lives?

- **How is that baby doing, whose birth you all celebrated two years ago now that the major exploration stage has arrived?**
- **How is the teenager doing that you heard was off to university in another part of the country?**
- **Has the renovation, that plagued the employee last year, been completed?**
- **Has the elderly parent, who caused so much concern, moved in with the family or settled into a nursing home?**

Just how connected are you to your people? What steps have you taken to stay in touch with the things important to them? How well do you really know them? What gets them excited? What causes them to fret or worry?

The first step, as in most other things, is to show the way. Telling a little about yourself, about your own life, your problems and joys, allows others to do likewise.

The leader, who talks about a new hobby they have taken up, will find they begin to hear about employees' interests outside of work. The leader who expresses concern about an ageing parent who lives out of town will hear from employees who have had or are dealing with similar circumstances. The leader who talks about his or her personal life says, in essence, I want you to know me as a person, beyond the one you see at work.

This "opening up" creates an atmosphere where people feel free to talk about things they are happy, sad or worried about, which, in turn, enables others to provide support. Support is the common element found in all companies who nurture and create a safe environment where people can make their best contribution.

The home renovation, the sailing trip, the back-packing excursion, the leaking hot water tank or the lost dog will all lead to conversations that pull people together. The ramifications of all this open and free exchange of information are often more supportive working relationships.

- **How can you help and support an employee when you know so little about what's worrying them?**
- **Can you laugh and enjoy their excitement about the trip they plan to take with their grandchildren?**

- **What will you say when you see them ill week after week and they have not felt comfortable enough to tell you about the crisis they are facing?**

In reality, the open and free exchange of information builds a camaraderie that would not otherwise exist.

The leader who wants to build a culture that nurtures the person will look at the services available in the place of employment or close by in the community and encourage employee participation if appropriate. Perhaps you have a Family and Employee Assistance Program where an employee can seek confidential help. Or the local community college or high school may have programs to educate and guide employees who require a bit of extra assistance to deal with some troubling aspect of their lives.

Nurturing and helping an employee doesn't have to be solely directed at problems; simply talking about community events they might enjoy will be all that is required. Sometimes services and events are more evident in small communities where the major employer has often built the recreation center, funded the playground at the local park, created the baseball diamond or sponsored the little league. But it doesn't have to stop at small communities. Certainly the big-city life, with employees dispersed in houses, apartments and condos over a wide geographic area, tends to make it harder to forge a sense of community, but it's not impossible.

The annual company golf tournament, the Christmas party or the staff mid-summer picnic can all be managed with some commitment and effort. The effective leader, committed to building and maintaining a strong feeling of belonging within the work unit, finds a way to be involved. He or she may lead a company committee devoted to social planning, or toss the pancakes for a pre-work breakfast, or cook the hamburgers for the "lunch in the plaza."

The leader may well support a social committee within his or her work unit to make sure the team plays from time to time. Perhaps a pizza is arranged for a lunch hour or a special needy family is "adopted" at Christmas and a hamper is filled. At other times perhaps a theme is introduced and everyone wears something red on Valentine's Day, or each person brings in a baby photo for the "guess who" contest. In other words, while the leader may not champion these activities he or she will certainly be involved and not remain aloof from the fun.

However, the balance between fun and work must be maintained and the leader will make sure employees know that "stealing" a little bit of time may be okay occasionally. But the work is the real reason everyone is here. Projects must be completed, clients must be served and goals have to be met. In other words, work must continue in a professional manner. Without a concerted effort to achieve goals, meet targets and accomplish planned activities there would be no team, there would be no work to come to, there would be no funds for special things; there might not even be a business. So, by all means, help the team have fun, but keep their eyes and yours clearly on the business and make it a success story, one they can be proud of.

A story about Nurturing

The unionized employees from a logging company in a small community were out on strike in the middle of winter and the bitterly cold weather was making it particularly hard for the people on the picket line.

The snow fell day after day and the wind whistled around the people as they paced up and down with their picket signs. The picketers had set up a small fire to ward off the bitter cold and some of them were huddled around it while others stamped their feet and sipped warm drinks.

The leader of the company was seen driving to work then getting out of his car and spending some time talking with the employees who were walking up and down outside the gate or clustered round their small fire pit.

After a few moments he got back in his car and went into the plant.

Later that morning the leader asked that some firewood be sent out to the men so they could keep warm while they "sat out the strike." When asked by some of the supervisors, if he was 'out of his mind' he replied,

"These are our employees, they are our neighbors. Our children go to school with their children, we shop in the same stores, work out at the same gym. After this strike is all over they will be back here working alongside us. Why wouldn't I make sure they are as comfortable as possible?"

He continued by saying,

"We may not see eye-to-eye on many points, yet I know in time we will reach an agreement. In the meantime, I've seen and heard about their discomfort and I'm in a position to do something about it, so I will."

Open

Not shut, allowing passage, generous, available, frank, concealing nothing in the mind, to reveal, to enlighten.

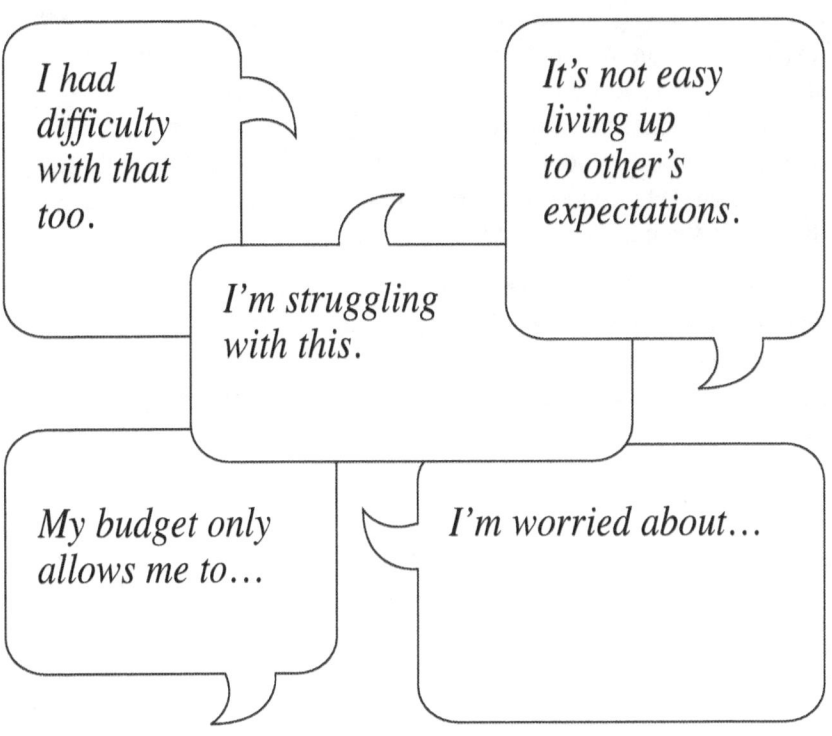

Open leadership is an emerging and growing trend. As a leader you know how important it is to be seen as credible in the eyes of your employees, to be respected, understood and able to influence others. But did you know that the leaders who have established just such a reputation believe it's also important to create an open and transparent working environment? These leaders understand that to truly connect with others, to have them believe in their intentions, and actions, they must first and foremost build an open and trusting atmosphere. But, and this is a huge but... it's essential to trust the messenger or the people won't trust the message.

Effective leaders know the value of letting others know more about their point of view, their knowledge, their fears, their interests, and their challenges. They get to know the people working for them in a way that fosters greater harmony and builds stronger working relationships.

The open leader will make sure that employees are provided with current information that will enable them to do their best work. Instead of giving their employees just what they need to know, the "open leader" generally gives so much more. Time and again they provide the inside scoop from meetings they attend, or the financial figures that allow employees to watch costs. They make sure their staff is given access to information that traditionally is kept within the management ranks. These leaders do all of this without divulging confidential information, yet provide as much as they possibly can. In return they usually find employees are able to make better decisions.

The effective leader knows it's important to open up and let others see who they really are, the real person, the one with true-to-life dilemmas just like everyone else – the man or woman behind the title. This does not mean that leaders have to let their private lives be wide open to scrutiny, but it does mean being frank, honest and real – being willing to be vulnerable while being professional. And, yes, you can merge the two!

Admit it; it's not always easy being in the leader's shoes. Some days you will sail though work and others will seem to be full of stumbling blocks and dilemmas. You're human, with strengths, abilities and skills. You have weaknesses, problems and lack of knowledge too. Some times you'll be right on the mark and other days solutions will prove to be elusive and trying.

On the home front you may have other challenges and things to juggle; a new home to settle in to, a son or daughter heading off to university, an aging parent unable to cope with life at home. Life is a balancing act. When leaders let their staff know that in many ways leaders are just like them, it frequently eliminates a lot of the pressures from the job.

As a leader you are not suddenly super-human. Leaders, experienced and novices alike, have roller coaster, up-and-down days. They feel energized and enthusiastic one moment then deflated and despondent the next. In other words, they are just like the employees who report to them.

The leader who is able, and willing, to say "I've never come across that before", doesn't appear un-informed. Instead, this willingness to share an insight into their background shows honesty. What makes a leader appear stupid or to lack credibility is pretending to know something, or being unable or unwilling to ask for information and help.

The leader who is willing to show their vulnerability, their foibles, and their lack of experience, and can even ask for help and input, will be richly rewarded. Here, the employees will say, is a "real" person, who also happens to be our leader.

Leaders who are willing to ask for help, demonstrate that learning is a continual and constant activity. The leader who is willing to pass on important information is saying, I trust you with this information and believe it's also important for you to know this.

The leader who is able to say "I'm not very good at this yet" acknowledges to others that it's okay to make some errors as it takes time to develop skills and become masterful. The leader who is willing to ask for guidance with some work challenge will gain their employees' respect far quicker than the one who believes it's important to look as if they have their career completely under control.

The open, free exchange of information may start anywhere but if the leader initiates it, makes the first move, it will help to create the atmosphere for others to do likewise. When there's an open and honest provision of information a tremendous amount of learning takes place and with it the ability to really connect with others.

So, being the leader doesn't mean being aloof, being error-free or being cautious. It means being able to let others "be real" in your presence by "being real" too.

A story about Open

A group of five independent consultants who were working with a client met one day to work together on a significant change about to be implemented in the organization. Each of these five people had previously worked with the client on a variety of projects, but none of them had met or worked together.

The client had begun a highly beneficial ritual at the start of each day of having a "check in" with his staff. The "check in", was a 30 second *"how are you doing"*, and *"what might be on your mind that will affect your ability to work"* conversation.

The results of this approach were comments like:

- *I needed to take my father to the nursing home this morning and I'm worried about how he's settling in.*
- *I feel great I lost 3 pounds.*
- *The project is right on track.*
- *My project file is missing. Has anyone seen it? or*
- *I need time to work on my notes for the presentation tomorrow.*

In other words, this "check in" gave everyone a chance to let others know why they might be seen checking their watch during the meeting, making phone calls to nursing homes, or hunting and rummaging for things on their desk. The "check in" stopped people from "second guessing" others' actions or moods.

The client suggested that, since the consultants would be working together for some time on this project, and as they hadn't worked together before, the "check in" activity might be a valuable way for the consultants to start each workday. The consultants looked a bit surprised but decided to give it a try.

The first attempt proved to be somewhat tentative, but valuable nevertheless, and created a "buzz" in the room as they realized they had learned a new technique, which could prove helpful with other clients. The next day, just as they were about to get down to work, one consultant reminded the group about the "check in" and they quickly gave their 30-second comment. By the end of the week the atmosphere in the room was quite different. Some people were providing support for things which would not normally have been discussed among these people. They found that being open and showing a bit of themselves had led to a stronger bond between the team which in turn led to a more cohesive working environment among the consultants.

A B C
D E F G
H I J K
L M N O
P Q R S
T U V W
X Y Z

Praise

Express warm approbation, commend the merits of, and extol the attributes of, to speak of with approval or admiration.

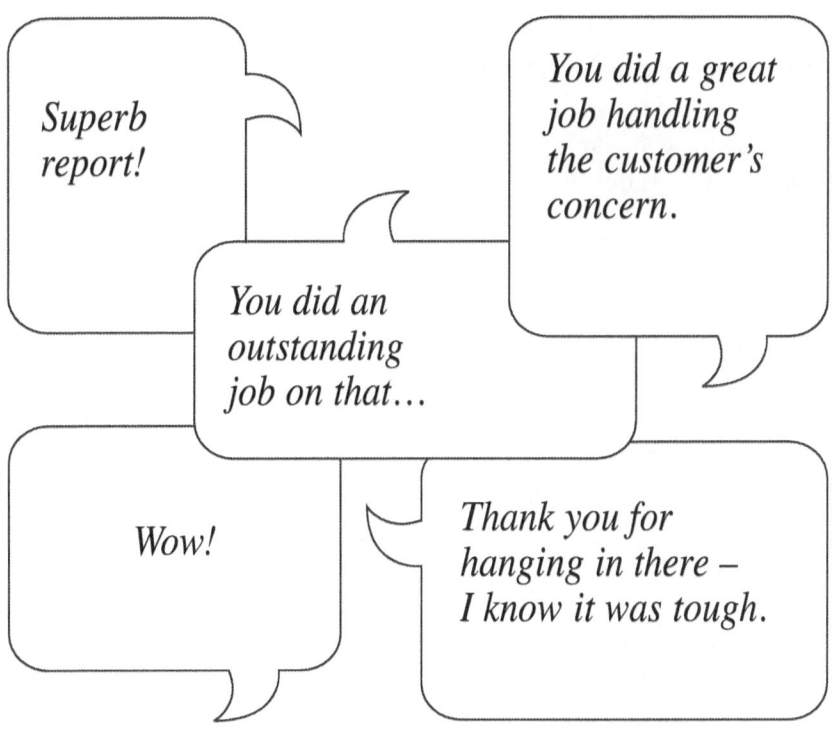

Pat someone on the back or give a word of praise and you'll realize from their reaction just how seldom this simple act occurs. There's nothing quite like some acknowledgment for a contribution that's been made, to give a spring to your step, a smile to your lips and a glow to your heart. Yet far too often people focus too much and for too long on the things they didn't manage to complete, the projects that went over budget, the meetings where discord arose, or the times they didn't listen.

But what about all of the things that go well day after day, month after month, year after year? What about the people you meet, who, when they walk out of your office, feel better, from having talked with you? Or those times you run great and productive meetings in spite of divergent points of view? Do you stop and reflect on those accomplishments to the same degree as the ones that cause angst? Probably not.

It's sad to say but the vast majority of employees we talked with told us their supervisor was quick to point out problems and talk about their mistakes, while the things they did, that went well, or caused no concern at all, were completely taken for granted, without so much as a word of encouragement or appreciation.

This does not mean that a leader should spend their day going around dishing out praise while overlooking the problems. It is, however, about balancing the communication, talking about the accomplishments and results as well as the outstanding issues.

It's natural to dwell on problems; it's a human thing, and some time **should** be spent looking back over what occurred to see what could be learned from the experience. But most leaders forget that just as much can be learned from an examination of the times when work proceeded smoothly, when deadlines were met, or when budgets came under the estimate and when employees pitched in and helped each other meet a client's special request.

- **What occurred to make it all jell?**
- **Which areas were given the most attention and how did that focus contribute to the end result?**
- **What did you personally do this time that could have made all the difference?**
- **Why was this particular meeting so much more productive that the one last week with the same people?**

The time spent looking at each success enables learning to take place – just as much as from a post mortem of the problem areas.

For some leaders, giving praise is a natural and straightforward thing to do, while others believe that employees know themselves when they've done a good job and all this "patting on the back" is unnecessary. Yet research shows that positive feedback not only gives that momentary feeling of pleasure, but also has long-lasting benefits. These benefits may continue for several days, leading to not only a happier but a more productive employee.

The ramifications of giving a word or two of acknowledgement often extend far beyond the actual recipient. Employees who are working alongside a colleague whose work has been praised may find that employee's pleasure "rubbing off" so to speak, generating a more harmonious working environment. Likewise, the employee who knows their work is appreciated may be a happier family member and, once again, some of their joy can rub off. This does not mean that leaders should go around scattering praise like a wedding guest with a handful of confetti. Praise has to be earned. And when offered it must be sincere and specific. "Thank you" is NOT enough.

- **What exactly made it a great job?**
- **What in particular did this employee do to make a difference?**
- **Why was this contribution so important?**
- **How did it further the goals of the organization?**
- **Why are you choosing this particular thing to acknowl**edge?

Praise has to be thoughtful, specific and tailored to the recipient. Unlike the wording on school report cards, which use standard phrases selected from an approved list, the careful and conscientious leader makes an effort to give praise that recognizes the employee's unique contribution.

Giving praise means first and foremost being observant to the facts, to read the letter of commendation, to listen to the customer who calls to express their delight with some service. It's hard to provide positive feedback in the absence of facts. Noticing what people do and how they do it will provide you with numerous opportunities to admire an approach, give thanks for an extra service or appreciate reliable work.

Finding the right time may mean never giving praise. So don't make a big deal out of it, there's really no need to find a quiet office and make an appointment to talk. A simple "thank you" in passing, while mentioning the specific activity you value, may be all that's required. It's worth mentioning that some employees like the quiet, private acknowledgement while others prefer some fanfare and public recognition. Make sure you consider the employee's style and manner before giving any public praise or, instead of making an employee feel grateful for the recognition, they may, want the ground to open up and swallow them! So always consider the most appropriate way to show the person you value their contribution.

Also, it's appropriate to match any gift or token of appreciation to the accomplishment and the individual. If an employee has worked hard and their efforts have saved the company $10,000, a box of chocolates is hardly appropriate. The acknowledgement must be suitable and tied to the employee's interests and hobbies. In some cases companies include a spouse in the recognition, especially if the extra work has meant less time with the family. Some examples in these cases might include a dinner for two at a fine restaurant, a week-end at a hotel, a spa or fitness package, or a round of golf and dinner for two.

Here's an interesting thought. Imagine you are attending your retirement dinner and one by one your colleagues stand up and talk about the impact you have made on them and their own careers. What legacy did you leave? What praise is being showered on you? What have you been doing to earn such accolades? Did you hear any of these wonderful comments **during** your career?

Now ponder your own actions. Have you been waiting to give praise, waiting for that special occasion, waiting so the timing is just right? Perhaps there is an opportunity to provide some acknowledgement right now – today – this minute.

So next time you see something that you are pleased about, take the time to let your employees know you do not take them for granted and that you value their contribution.

A story about Praise

A young and inexperienced leader, working in a large, industrial, unionized facility, liked to talk with the employees about their work. He wanted them to recognize that their attention made a difference to the quality of the product. He was ridiculed, however, by his more-seasoned colleagues who considered him "too soft'" with all of his praise and talk about "nice stuff."

The young man steadfastly believed it was the right thing to do and, in spite of the laughs and jibes from his co-workers, continued to thank people for their good work.

Over time his colleagues noticed that whenever he was on shift the production was higher, safety issues were non-existent and employee relations were harmonious. They wondered what he was doing that was different from them. Did he have an older, more experienced crew? Perhaps the production runs were not as complex? Maybe there was something special going on that made everyone so happy? Was he bringing in pizza or giving them something extra as a reward? In other words, they looked everywhere for the things that could account for the differences occurring under his supervision. He assured them he didn't have anything special going on; all he did was let the crew know how much he appreciated them. They could not, and would not, accept that this alone could be making such a difference.

This young man walked around the shop floor and chatted casually to everyone making sure he had something special to say to every single employee; he let them know he was glad they were there. This was totally foreign to the employees, who were not accustomed to this style. Initially they brushed off his comments and seemed embarrassed about it. However, this young man knew that being recognized and appreciated was a core need, and so he pressed on.

In time the men who worked for him began to enjoy his visits and they opened up and talked about a wide range of topics. The young man soon attracted attention in the company and was promoted again and again until he became the manager in a large plant. To this day, in a plant with over 900 employees, he still walks around talking with people; and is a highly regarded leader.

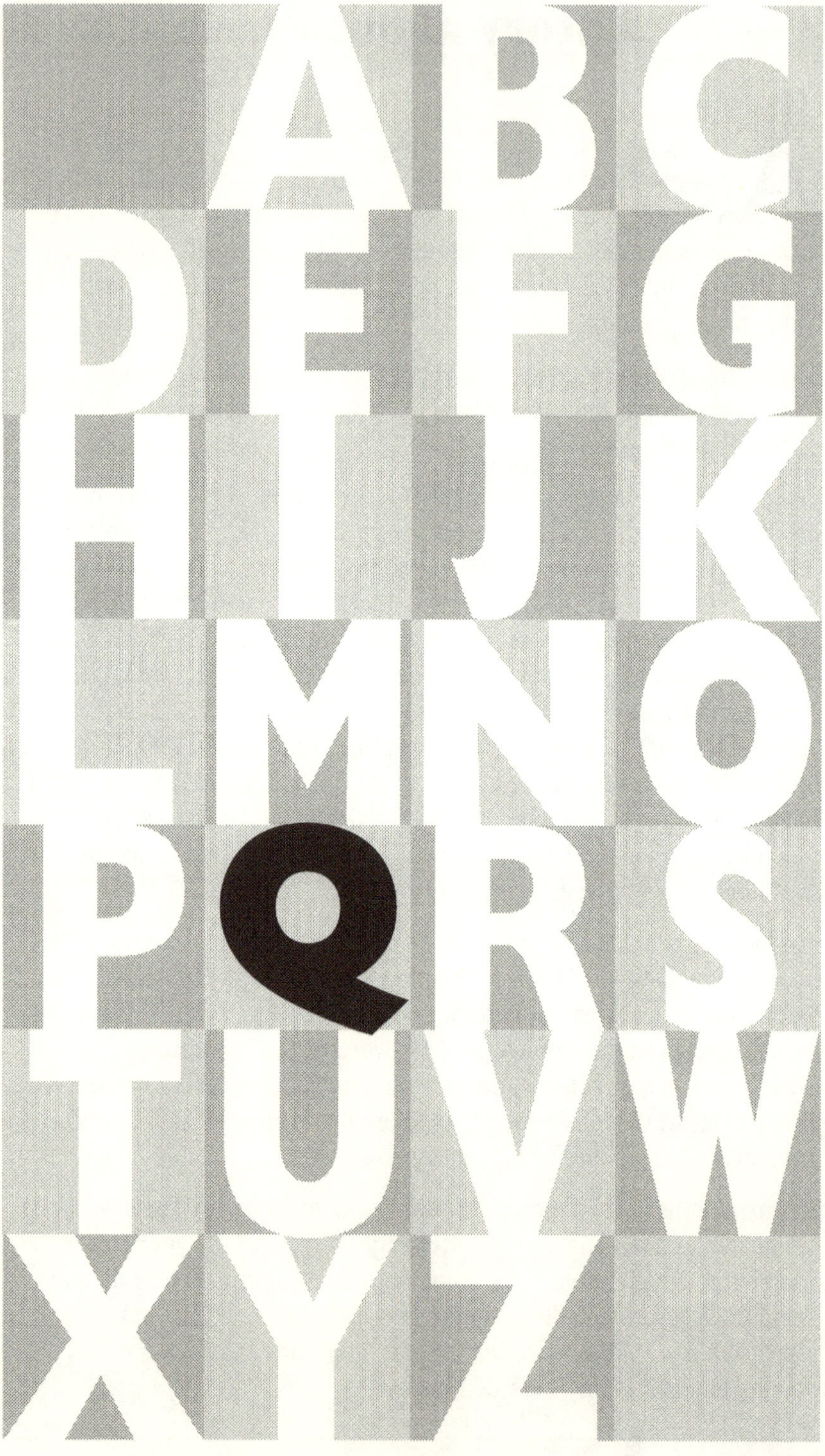
ABC
DEFG
HIJK
LMNO
PQRS
TUVW
XYZ

Questions

A word phrase or sentence asking about a particular point, fact, etc., designed to test knowledge, a means to elicit an answer, seek information.

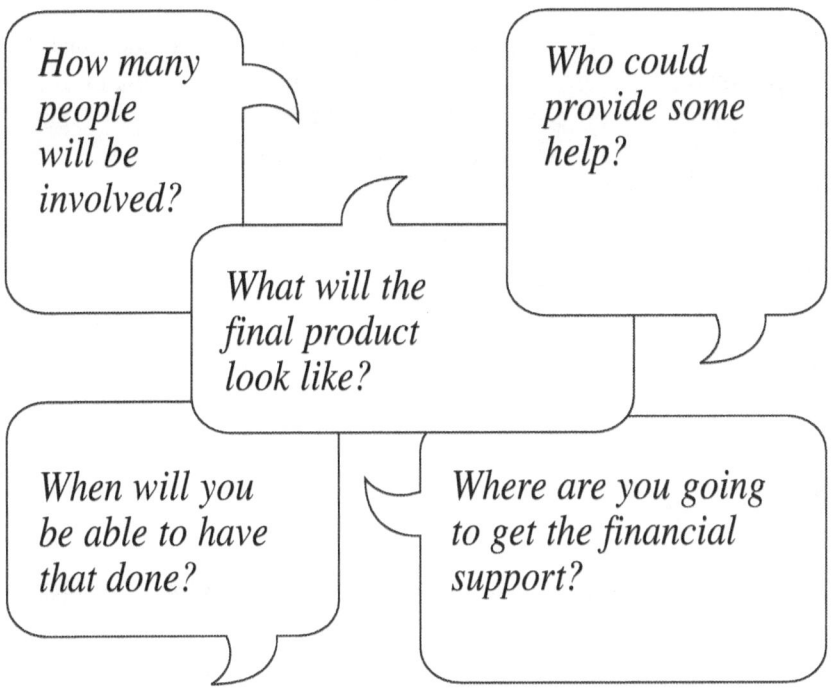

How many people will be involved?

Who could provide some help?

What will the final product look like?

When will you be able to have that done?

Where are you going to get the financial support?

Questioning how you do things and which processes can enable your operation to grow can be the start of significant improvements. However, there is an art to asking questions without appearing like an interrogator and the wise and skillful leader, would be well advised to develop some skill in this area.

Often it's the leaders in the organization who are subjected to a litany of questions. The knock on the door may be an employee seeking advice as they struggle with some dilemma. Or perhaps it's the manager who wants to know about a project's progress and has a multitude of questions. Or maybe it's the customer who has not been pleased with some service and will want to know what steps are being taken to correct their problem.

So the leader's job often looks like answer, answer, answer, all day long. While giving answers is important asking the right questions is even more so.

There are many types of questions and they all provide astonishingly different results. Knowing which type of question to apply to the situation is what makes a leader more effective.

There are some questions that we call "open." Open-ended questions are designed to encourage someone to speak and give more than just a word or two in response. The leader who asks for an employee's input on issues or proposals, will stimulate a more motivated workforce from the simple act of asking for ideas and input.

Open-ended questions generally start with the five "Ws" and an "H." These key opening words are:

- **what**
- **why**
- **where**
- **when**
- **who** and
- **how**

If you start a question with any of these words it's impossible to receive an answer with a "Yes" or "No." Open-ended questions are used to establish rapport, seek additional information, encourage generation of possible solutions or to explore and draw out more information.

heatherconsults@shaw.ca **L is for Leader**

Open-ended questions are invaluable for the leader who wants to develop the skills of the employees who come knocking at their door. Next time an employee says, "How do I do...?" or "What do you think I should do with...?" or "Can you tell me what I should do with...?" consider asking open questions instead of jumping in with a ready answer.

If you ask your employees to tell you what they have considered and then continue exploring other directions, you can lead them to look at possible consequences of following their initial path. By engaging them in a line of questioning on a regular basis your employees will learn much more than by simply listening and going off to do as you say.

Who else have you discussed this with and what was their reaction?

What will be the major hurdles you anticipate if we proceed?

When will we be able to move ahead?

Where are the other facts to support this decision?

Why do you think this is the best approach?

How do you want to pass on the information to our clients?

The goal for every leader should be to develop the expertise of their employees and there can be no better way than to **stop answering questions and start asking them.**

However, in order for the questions to be well received it is worth paying attention to the tone and manner of the asking, as much as the questions themselves. Questions asked in a manner that implies lack of thought will certainly not endear you to your employees. Asking in a supportive and considerate manner is essential for deep and conscious learning and to increase the likelihood of further coaching.

Recall what it's like to feel some doubt and uncertainty about an action and how talking things over with a mentor or peer can be so enlightening. This is how your employees feel. Sometimes just the act of "talking out loud to someone" clears the head and makes the decision so much easier. Nobody likes to feel incompetent, yet requiring assistance and looking for guidance or an attentive ear is an indicator that this employee needs reassurance and help. Be gentle, firm and reassuring whenever possible and strive to "ask'" rather than "tell."

Questions for Probing or Learning More

To probe into another person's line of thinking you can ask questions that begin like this:

- *To what extend to you feel...?*
- *How do you feel about...?*
- *What are your views on...?*
- *In what way does...?*
- *To what degree do you think...?*
- *If that's the case, what would be your approach to...?*

These questions will give you a greater insight into how another person thinks and makes decisions.

Asking these deep and probing questions is of immense value at work; questions such as these really make the person think through the various issues or problems. In some cases by asking the right question you expose something that was not even considered. At other times the answers you get will lead you, to consider a different viewpoint. Employees who have found themselves subjected to a supportive and careful line of questioning often mention how it has helped them take on more responsibility, and increased their self-confidence as well.

The leader who diligently pursues this approach will find employees no longer come knocking at the office door seeking answers, but will, in most cases, have done some thinking and may even have considered potential solutions.

In time you may even find your employees telling you about decisions they have made and the line of self-questioning they used to reach their decision. It's then that you'll know that all of the time you spent asking questions has really paid off.

A story about Questions

An airline company was experiencing problems with lost or damaged baggage. Disgruntled customers were upset when faced with delays in being compensated. Letters were received demanding action and they needed to be answered. In the meantime employees were taking days off due to stress or were handling things in a way that only added to the customers' frustration.

In the past this situation would have been managed with a "train and it will go away" mindset. The employees would have been sent to a course on how to deal with difficult customers or even a "stress course" to help them manage the work-related problems. The organization would have had to fill the jobs while their staff was away and find replacements for the days employees were absent. In short the budget would have been stretched beyond expectations.

However, the management of this airline decided it was time to take another approach. They decided to ask questions and truly listen to the answers. They took a close look at what was creating this untenable situation.

They asked employees who handled customers at the baggage counter what their main complaints were. Slow payments, was the number one issue. The management explored this complaint and found there were seven steps and seven different people involved to processes the check for the customer.

They then began to ask
- *Why do we do it this way?*
- *What could we do to streamline the entire process?*
- *What challenges could arise from doing it this way?*

And, so on.

In time they came up with a radically new way to process payments by providing the front-line employees with the information they needed to look up suitcase models and current replacement costs. They even provided a cheque-printing machine at the counter.

The result of this in-depth enquiry, combined with open minds ready to listen to some new ideas, led to many dramatic and unprecedented changes. The employees, instead of being stressed, found they could now help the customers immediately and that they were thanked more often than they were complained to! Some people still complained, but a great many of the letters they began to receive said how much the customers appreciated the prompt way their problems were dealt with.

In short, this company went on to encourage its leaders to probe into other "habitual ways of working" to find new opportunities for growth and problem solving.

Questioning, rather than making quick and somewhat superficial decisions, became the way of life for everyone in the organization and contributed to many innovative changes.

Results

Consequence, issue, outcome of something. The effect of something, the success or benefit obtained from a course of action.

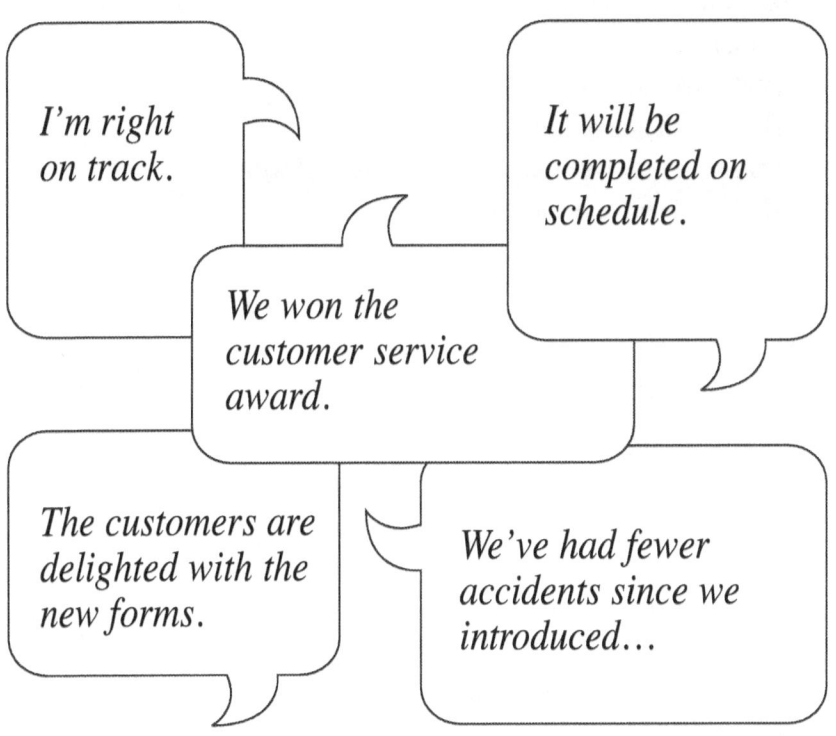

I'm right on track.

It will be completed on schedule.

We won the customer service award.

The customers are delighted with the new forms.

We've had fewer accidents since we introduced...

R ight on! Great! Even though everyone fundamentally knows that results are important, there are a great many leaders who are entirely satisfied when their employees "try" to make a difference.

In a workshop I led, I placed a big, but empty, box on the floor and asked one of the participants to try to pick it up. When he swiftly lifted it from the floor I smilingly admonished him by saying, "I didn't ask you to pick it up, I just asked you to try." He looked at me, grinned and walked back to his seat ready for the lesson that followed.

The lesson was based on the concept that we are either doing something – creating a result – or we are not. Trying is not a result, period!

Yet time after time well-intentioned leaders "reward" the employee who says they are trying even though no tangible results that can be seen, measured or quantified. Results matter. In fact, they are crucial for a business to thrive and grow.

So when employees tell their leader that they are "trying," it's important for the leader to probe, to drill down, and find out exactly what they have done.

- **What have they accomplished?**
- **What results have they created?**
- **What progress was made toward the established goal**
- **What parts have been completed?**
- **How far are they towards reaching the target?**

The leader who wants tangible results examines the sustained activity and ensures results are being made.

Businesses are successful because the employees are creating RESULTS.

The leaders who ask their employees

- *What are you working on today?*
- *Do you need any support from me in reaching your goal?*
- *What might derail your plans?*
- *What progress did you make on…?*
- *What is your next step?*
- *When can you show me the work that's been completed to date?*
- *What contingency plans have you considered?*

■ *How confident are you that you'll be able to complete the job today?*

will certainly make it clear that reaching goals and creating results matter.

Repetitive actions always form the bulk of any job, but without keeping a close eye on the expected results, the routine tasks often lead to the employee being side-tracked, with time being spent on unproductive activities. If you want results, you must ensure employees focus on the outcomes they need to create. They have to know what's important, and be informed of any shifts in priorities as they occur, so they can realign their actions in accordance with the goals that have been established.

Let's look at an example. If a leader says reducing employee turnover by 25% within the next six months is desired, then it's obvious that a clearly established, measurable result has been identified. Following on this, background work needs to take place that will help establish some parameters for the future activities.

■ **What is the current percentage of staff turnover?**
■ **Why are employees leaving?**
■ **What policies might be contributing to the problem?**
■ **Are there policies that impede career advancement?**
■ **What about training and opportunities to learn?**

Perhaps these questions will lead to further scrutiny so that internal policies or practices are examined in detail, enabling the leader and the employees to take a fresh look at the entire staffing process.

To reach their goal a strategy will have to be formed that will substantially change the way employees are hired, supported, given career growth opportunities, provided feedback, etc.

In other words, once the result has been firmly established, specific actions must be identified so employees can take action to ensure the result is made. The result will not happen just because you want it to.

A story about Results

A major government department launched an innovative effort that was expected to accelerate the development of the next generation of leaders. The participants were drawn mostly from the ranks of middle managers, different business units and functional areas. Leadership development activities included group mentoring, individual assessments, development planning, a leadership workshop and work on strategic business projects.

I was asked to assist with their initiative. Face-to-face coaching was considered a key enabler for this approach to leadership development because participants could work privately with their coach to develop specific competencies.

The coaching agreement was prepared in conjunction with the new leader and the leader's immediate supervisor. The leader and his supervisor agreed on the competencies, crucial for future growth so they would be in a position to assess progress.

The coach/leader meetings were created specifically to develop behaviors that were visible and measurable – the leader wanted his supervisor to notice the changes by observing him in action doing things differently.

The coach/leader relationship continued over a three-month period and each week the leader and I established one or two very detailed and specific concepts or skills to apply.

Our weekly meetings consisted of a report from the leader on the application of the new approach and the reactions or results that emerged. Frequently we discussed alternatives, role-played and fine tuned approaches, so the leader could develop expertise. The leader also provided a tool for his supervisor to use to track the differences that he observed and the impact those adjustments made to his overall effectiveness.

By staying focused on key, specific, measurable results, the leader was able to make significant progress. In time the leader's observation skills improved. He noticed his supervisor had a particular way of communicating and he was able to adapt his own style to ensure that conversations between them stayed on track.

This leader was so impressed with the progress he made each week that he encouraged his own employees to work with a coach for their own personal development. Later, his supervisor commented that the results had been dramatic and had been sustained even when the workload had increased significantly.

ABC
DEFG
HIJK
LMNO
PQRS
TUVW
XYZ

Safety

The condition of being safe from risk or danger. The quality or state of not presenting or involving risk or danger. Freedom from danger or injury.

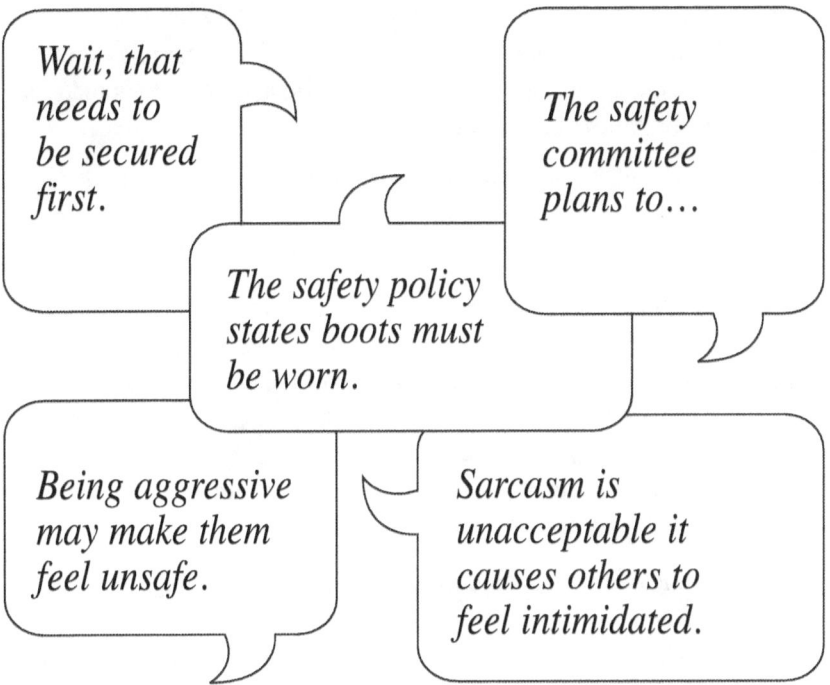

Wait, that needs to be secured first.

The safety committee plans to…

The safety policy states boots must be worn.

Being aggressive may make them feel unsafe.

Sarcasm is unacceptable it causes others to feel intimidated.

Some leaders consider safety only in the context of physical safety and no one disputes the fact that maintaining employee safety must be of paramount importance. But another type of safety is often overlooked – psychological safety. This is the type that makes it impossible to speak out when the employee's opinion is different from the leader, or when the team wants to head in one direction and they are ridiculed when they speak in favor of another option. Safety in both physical and psychological areas must be maintained for employee well being.

The leader in an industrial setting, with machinery and other major pieces of equipment, is constantly bombarded with safety concerns and regulations. The Workers' Compensation Board, the local safety council or specific industrial bodies all have regulations regarding the safe operation of equipment, safe storage and keeping of supplies, use of hazardous chemicals, use of scaffolding or working around asbestos and so on. The regulations and information flow to and from the workplace in response to accidents, near misses and fatalities.

In some organizations there is a position dedicated specifically to employee health and safety, someone who is intimately involved in all aspects of safety as it relates to their workplace. Their role is to know the regulations that apply to their industry, toxic and hazardous material handling, ergonomics and so forth.

Unfortunately, many leaders see this person in a different light – as the one who is "responsible" for the safety of the employees. This is not the case.

When an accident or injury occurs, the person who is actually held accountable is the immediate supervisor – the leader of the work team. This is the person who assigned the work, ensured the trainee received sufficient knowledge to complete the work, assessed their capabilities, and is held accountable for the results. So it's of paramount importance that every leader understands the requirements and regulations that apply to their people.

The effective leader makes sure time is spent understanding the safety requirements and ensures employees know they must adhere to the regulations. This might entail spending time with a fire marshal, meeting with someone from the safety council, or some other agency or governing body that takes care of employee health and safety.

The leader must ensure each employee is trained in the safe working procedures. In addition, detailed records must be kept that show this training has taken place and the employee's skills have been assessed.

Far too many men and women suffer needlessly because of workplace injuries. This often results in life-changing situations requiring long-term care or major re-training to adapt to a career change. In some tragic cases fatalities occur and family life is never the same.

The effective leader never wants to find himself or herself undergoing in-depth interrogation about the facts leading up to an injury or death. The leader who cares about their employees' welfare makes sure adequate safety measures are taken and that employees know they can refuse to work if they feel their personal safety is in jeopardy.

The leader who takes safety seriously will **always** wear a hard hat in an industrial setting, **never** drive without wearing a seat belt, **always** use a ladder to reach something overhead, and **never** ask an employee to skip a safe way of doing the job in favor of speed or cost savings.

The other type of safety that we referred to earlier – psychological safety – is less tangible.

This safety is derived from solid, cooperative and pleasant working relationships between various individuals. It's free from intimidation, ridicule and name calling, and free from political, sexual, racial and gender discrimination.

Leaders can have a huge impact in this area by leading by example, establishing ground rules and immediately nipping any deviation in the bud. It's interesting that employees will often defend their actions by saying, *"it was in fun," "I was just kidding,"* or *"can't anyone make a joke around here anymore?"* Don't be fooled; psychological safety must be protected if you want to build a solid, hard-working team that supports each other.

The person who offends, teases, pokes fun at, or intimidates another must be corrected without delay. They must understand that this type of communication cannot, and will not, be tolerated in a professional, well-run workplace and will not be acceptable under your leadership at any time.

So, working safely, keeping employees within the boundaries of good work practices and following all regulations will go a long way towards making the workplace safe. Governing how you communicate, and making sure others guard against unprofessional language, will greatly help in fostering a tight, cohesive team built upon mutual respect.

A story about Safety

A new president and CEO of a large multi-national forestry company announced that safety would be his number one priority and that he expected nothing less from everyone in the company. The directors, mill mangers and others within the organization had heard it all before, from annual reports to meetings, so they didn't pay too much attention – at first.

The president and CEO decided that the best way to get to know this huge and diverse company would be to travel to some of the operations and attend some management meetings. He wanted to hear first-hand about some of the issues they were dealing with.

The manager in a large pulp mill told us later about the president's visit and how taken aback he had been at his forthright manner. The manager had circulated an agenda for the president's meeting to all senior department heads and set a date and time when everyone would be able to attend.

When everyone had assembled in the room the president asked the manager why he had made "safety" the third item on the agenda, when he thought he had made it perfectly clear that it was number one!

He went on to say that he expected to see safety given top billing in all meetings, project plans, hiring considerations, budget preparation, plant tours and conversations with every single employee to show they are committed to this end. He concluded with, "Do I make myself clear?"

You better believe he made an impact. The news spread quickly throughout the company about the correction that had been made. Yet, far more important was the result he created.

heatherconsults@shaw.ca **L** is for Leader

Safety did improve – dramatically.

People paid closer attention to fixing things that normally would have been left a little longer, they talked about safety at every meeting if only to touch base to make sure things were working well, and they wore the safety gear and followed the regulations to the letter.

Here was someone in the company's most senior position, someone not normally out wandering the grounds of mills and logging operations, someone who knew the power of action, who was committed to getting each and every employee home safely at the end of the day.

ABCDEFGHIJKLMNOPQRSTUVWXYZ

Teamwork

The quality whereby individuals unselfishly subordinate their own part to the general effort of the group with whom they are working or playing.

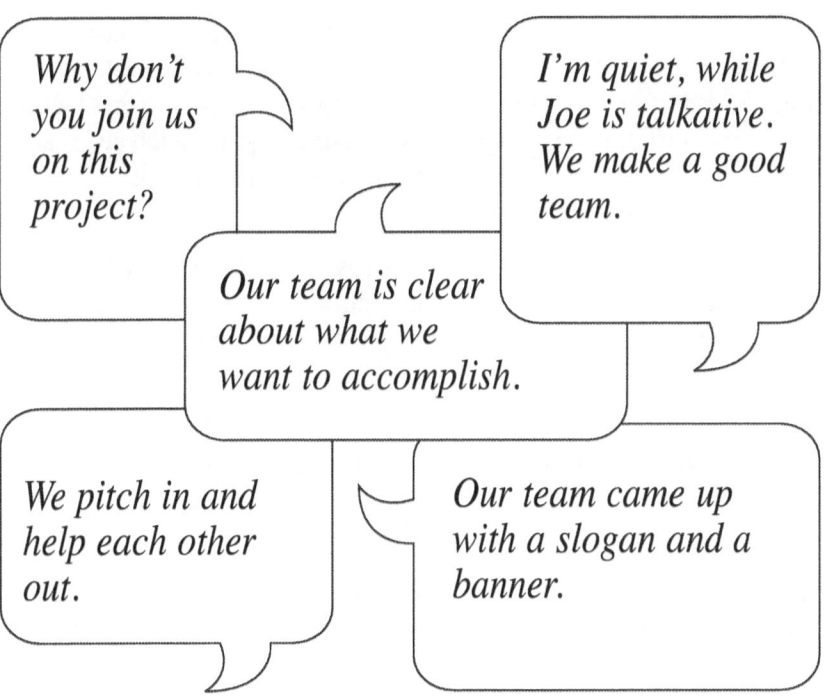

Why don't you join us on this project?

I'm quiet, while Joe is talkative. We make a good team.

Our team is clear about what we want to accomplish.

We pitch in and help each other out.

Our team came up with a slogan and a banner.

T eams are formed when there is a common purpose and each member is willing to put forth their ideas and best possible contribution to meet a pre-determined goal. A group of individuals working together does NOT make a team!

The same leaders who are often superbly gifted at working with individuals will struggle or seem to "fall apart" when faced with a group of people jostling to be heard. Teamwork is a totally different game to the one played out when it's just a one-on-one discussion.

When groups of people come together to plan and debate the pros and cons of proposed actions you can expect, and should indeed get, a healthy and animated discussion.

How to manage the discussion and the conflicting points of view is another matter, and a review of the section under "Boundaries" might help.

This is when the leader is called upon to facilitate the dialogue, to make sure everyone listens, to check understanding. He or she will paraphrase to ensure key ideas are captured and condense the essence, before setting the troops free to get on with the work.

But teamwork is not just about what happens in meetings, it's also about pulling together in the same direction. That's what leads to outstanding results. Leaders know that when a group of people come together there are bound to be different perspectives, unique communication styles and strong feelings. This is what makes teams work – it's all about "vive la différence," as the French would say.

In any group you're likely to find the analytical, detail-oriented types, the supportive and caring people, the controlling and directing people and the outgoing push-the-boundaries creative individuals.

In order to work well with these divergent styles the effective leader will seek out help in understanding the theory behind the different working styles and ensure the team is exposed to this theory too. Variety is the spice of life and it's variety that's the life blood of teams that excel.

The skilled leader will ensure that the team is comprised of the right mix for the project at hand. The analytical thinkers, who ponder and plan, are most suited to detailed work with facts and data to support decisions. While the controlling and directing types, who are generally most vocal in presenting a "this is what we should do now" stance, are

heatherconsults@shaw.ca **L** is for Leader

best suited to leading and organizing the work. Then there are the quiet, caring and supportive people who want harmony, sometimes it seems at all costs. These people are the cheerleaders, the helpful "behind the scenes" people, who make less visible contributions that often go unnoticed. Finally we come to the energetic, passionate and creative thinkers who see all sorts of possibilities; their participation is often to bring a fresh new perspective to the task. Since, these people often "think outside of the box" their creative energy needs to be channeled into a role where they can roll up their sleeves and get to work.

Can you imagine a team comprised of just one type? Just imagine a group of "directing types" jostling for control and you quickly realize that the variety of styles is really what makes teams work well.

The death knoll for teams is "superficial agreement," the quick and ready agreement without deep discussion and exploration into opposing points of view. If the group seems to reach a solution too quickly don't jump for joy instead, ask yourself, what might be preventing the team from sharing their opinions and challenging others' thought processes? The quick and smooth decision may well indicate an underlying belief of it not being "safe" to talk about a difference of opinion.

Perhaps you have a high number of reflective participants who need time to consider alternatives before speaking their mind. Or maybe there's a highly vocal and energetic participant whose confident style makes others feel inadequate and unsure. That's why understanding style differences can be so important for the group's cohesiveness.

Encourage the participants to talk about what they think effective teams go through to reach important goals and you might well find the topic of healthy conflict is brought up as a totally acceptable behavior. You can then ask the group how they plan to deal with differences of opinion so you can establish ground rules for this exchange of ideas.

If a group has come together from different work units to address a project, problem or plan, then there are predictable stages they will go through before they truly become a tight cohesive team.

The first stage is **Forming**, and is characterized by a high dependence on the leader for guidance and direction. Generally the leader must be prepared to answer many questions about the team's goals and the process for reaching them.

Later the team will move towards the stage known as **Storming**. This is when team members find that decisions don't come easily within the group. People vie for position as they attempt to establish themselves in relation to other team members. Cliques and splinter groups may form along with power struggles.

After this more disruptive stage passes, the team will reach the **Norming** stage. Here we find that participants generally respond well to the leader's facilitation. Sometimes, the entire group makes some of the bigger decisions, while individuals, charged with some special task, may make smaller decisions. The team seems to enjoy working together and usually has a lot of fun.

Lastly, the team reaches the **Performing** stage, when they operate in a highly independent manner without the need for intervention by the leader; they have clarity of purpose and self manage the work and distribution of tasks.

A story about Teamwork

Sharon Wood, the first Canadian woman to reach the summit of Everest, was heard speaking at a conference about how everyone on the climbing team made a contribution towards the goal of putting someone from their team on the summit.

She went on to speak eloquently about the roles and responsibilities of each member and how important each of them was to her ultimate success. There were the cooks who prepared the highly nutritious food that sustained them through the blizzards and their adjustment to the altitude. The cameramen who climbed with them and recorded the progress they made and life at base camp in all its ugly moments. There were people in charge of supplies, tents, or health care. All were acknowledged as she told her story of that long and arduous climb.

The leader of the expedition was a quiet person, unknown to most of us, his name seldom mentioned in regard to this great accomplishment. Stationed at base camp, he directed the flow of supplies, people and resources that created the seamless and constant flow of necessities that in turn enabled the climbers to climb.

Sharon spoke with gratitude about the team what worked tirelessly, diligently, and steadfastly, unseen by the cameras and out of the limelight that allowed the few chosen people to make that historic climb. Her success truly was realized because of the team who supported every aspect of this venture.

ABC
DEFG
HIJK
LMNO
PQRS
TUVW
XYZ

Unions

To organize into a trade union or unions, to cause to conform to rules.

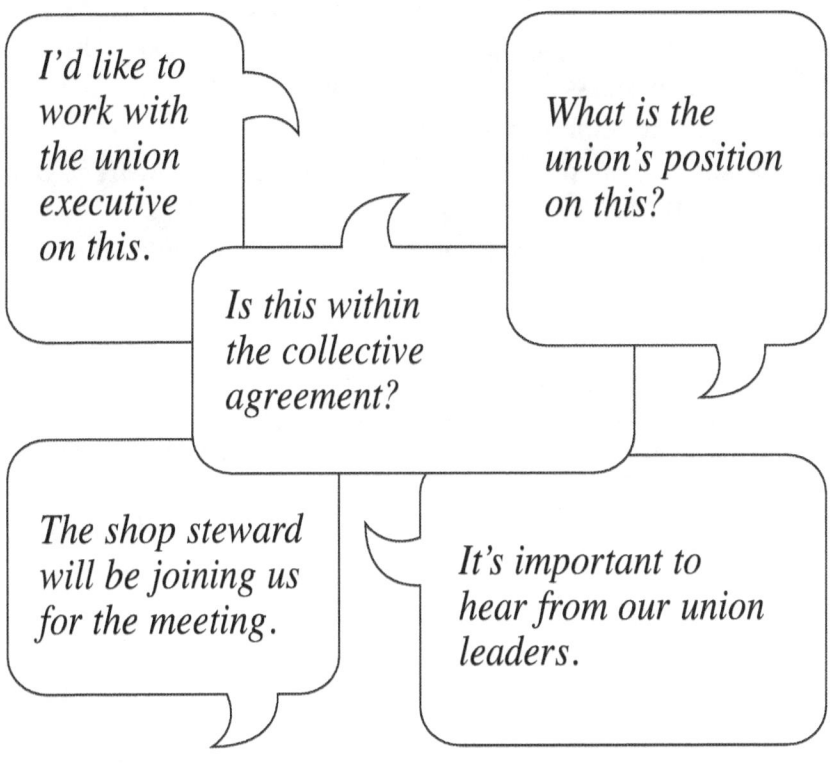

I'd like to work with the union executive on this.

What is the union's position on this?

Is this within the collective agreement?

The shop steward will be joining us for the meeting.

It's important to hear from our union leaders.

U nions are here to stay. Many organizations throughout the world have employees who are members of a bargaining unit or union. In some organizations the management team works well with the union executive and brings them into all manner of planning discussions, especially when the discussions will affect their members.

Yet, unfortunately, there are many more organizations where management-union relationships are cooler, fragmented and even hostile, focusing on opposing points of view and power struggles. When this occurs, the two sides take stances that make it hard for either one to back down. This results in a stalemate, which in turn may lead to a strike or lock out – something neither party really wants. Regrettably, top people on both sides are expected to show they are "in control", so appearing to "give in" is considered weak; and that it is certainly not something any leader wants for a reputation.

So how do some companies form strong bonds with the union executive? And how do these union executives justify the cozy relationship to their membership? What elements are present that bring the two sides together? It helps if they realize that they both have common goals:

- **To keep in business so everyone has a job.**
- **To make sure employees are safe.**
- **To ensure the company is profitable, so that employees are paid fairly for the work performed.**
- **To ensure employees are involved in decisions that affect them and their work.**

Once both parties realize they are on the same page, even have the same goals, the dialogue moves more smoothly. Yet reaching this point is frequently overlooked as the parties jostle for position over much smaller issues and forget to stand back and look at the larger picture. If they did it would become apparent that the small matter before them is really part of a much bigger issue and possibly something they both agree on.

When an employee seeks out help from a shop steward it's usually because the leader and the employee have had a miscommunication and have not been able to step back and try another angle. When the shop steward is brought in, he or she is often expected to defend the employee's side tooth and nail against the "management enemy!"

heatherconsults@shaw.ca **L is for Leader**

The wise leader will make every effort to work with an employee to find out what troubles them and listen attentively and seek options for addressing the concern. This does not mean that in every case the employee and manager will see eye-to-eye, but there is a much greater possibility if a concerted effort is made.

But how do leaders deal with chronic problems? For example, an employee who clearly doesn't care about coming to work and misses many days per month, or takes an hour for lunch instead of the half-hour? The leader is advised to follow the steps in the F-*feedback* section and document the commitments and action plans the employee and leader make.

What happens when the leader avoids these tough conversations and lets things slide? Generally other issues will surface – colleagues who work alongside the "problem" employee wonder why they *"get away with things"* and why the leader is *"not doing anything about it"*. The build-up of frustration leads to grumbling and discontent among the majority of the employees who are working hard. Soon morale has slipped, often along with work standards. Clearly, the situation demands quick action, including a timely conversation.

In cases where leaders overlook problem performance or make excuses, it frequently comes back to haunt them. At some point in time the employee will need to be talked to and may well reply, *"I've been doing this for a year and you've never said anything, so I took that to mean you were okay with it."*

If leaders press things and employees bring in the shop stewards, they are likely to hear the same rationale from the union executive. If the leader decides to seek advice from the labor relations department, it's probable they will be unable to offer help at this stage, as a precedent has been established.

The only action a leader can take is to make sure the employee now understands the expectations from this time forward. As leader you must make sure the expectations are met, or talked about immediately, if there's any deviation.

The best union/management relationships appear to occur when management is empowered to act, to invite and include the union to meetings, are confident they will be supported when they make decisions, can fine tune agreements and are trusted to apply sound judgment.

From the other side, a more harmonious working relationship seems to occur when the union executive is willing to work *with* the management team to provide workable ideas. This usually occurs when they are brought in to discussions early, long before a decision is made so they can truly be a partner in the process.

This partnering is more common than one might realize, and benefits everyone in the organization. Generally, both sides are actually on the same side! Finding the common ground usually ends up showing they have more in common than they both realized. It takes time to form a solid, stable working relationship, but it can be turned on its head if someone acts in an untrustworthy manner.

So to make an impact, and build a union/management team, will take time, great communication skills – especially listening –, and a willingness to compromise.

A story about Unions

A sawmill on the coast of British Columbia and a member of the International Woodworkers of America, had a reputation for producing a highly desirable product for its clients. This particular operation was head-and-shoulders above the other mills in the company and they took pride in the internal competition. On top of that, their employees were consistently winning national awards for their unique talents, which helped to make the plant so successful. Things were looking good.

The employees from all areas met on a regular basis to talk about ways to improve and stay ahead of the competition. They fine-tuned some processes, examined maintenance schedules and looked at their log supply in order to find ways to incrementally improve productivity. Yet over time this operation noticed that its major competitors were indeed catching up. Although they had a vision, a goal, to always be in the lead, the gap was closing.

The unionized employees and the management team met with me, as I had been working with them for the past four years looking for ways they could "notch" things up a bit more. At the meeting an employee mentioned that when a particular employee was on a certain job the production went up. Then another mentioned that the maintenance on a piece of equipment wasn't necessary as often when another employee was operating it. The team was curious. Then an employee made a radical suggestion: *"Why don't we set up video cameras to watch exactly what we all do that makes such a difference to the results? We might learn a thing or two."*

I waited to see the others' reactions and, much to my surprise, the group all agreed and then went on to talk about setting ground rules so it would work for everyone. It was agreed that people could volunteer to be taped and that when they watched the tapes there were to be no snide comments. No one was to make fun of what they saw. Finally, the tapes were to be erased immediately after being viewed, while everyone was still in the room.

A union employee was designated to propose this novel approach to the other employees who were not at the meeting, to see if they would go along with it. The answer was a resounding *"yes."* Soon a camera was brought in, people were taped and meetings were set up to see the results. I worked with the team to determine the best practices, and in time a whole new set of procedures was in place. The plant went on to achieve more records for production, safety and employee morale.

The union executive tried to jump in at one point to stop the video taping, but the members held their ground showing the process they had put in place to protect everyone. The union agreed to let this unorthodox approach continue and in the end took pride in what their members had accomplished.

The story of this outstanding group of employees, and this innovative and exceptional organization, spread and I was invited to speak at the Coaching and Mentoring Conference in the United Kingdom to tell the story of these courageous people, a task I was delighted to perform.

A B C
D E F G
H I J K
L M N O
P Q R S
T U V W
X Y Z

Vision

Act or faculty of seeing, sight, seen in a dream or trance, prophetic, thing seen in the imagination.

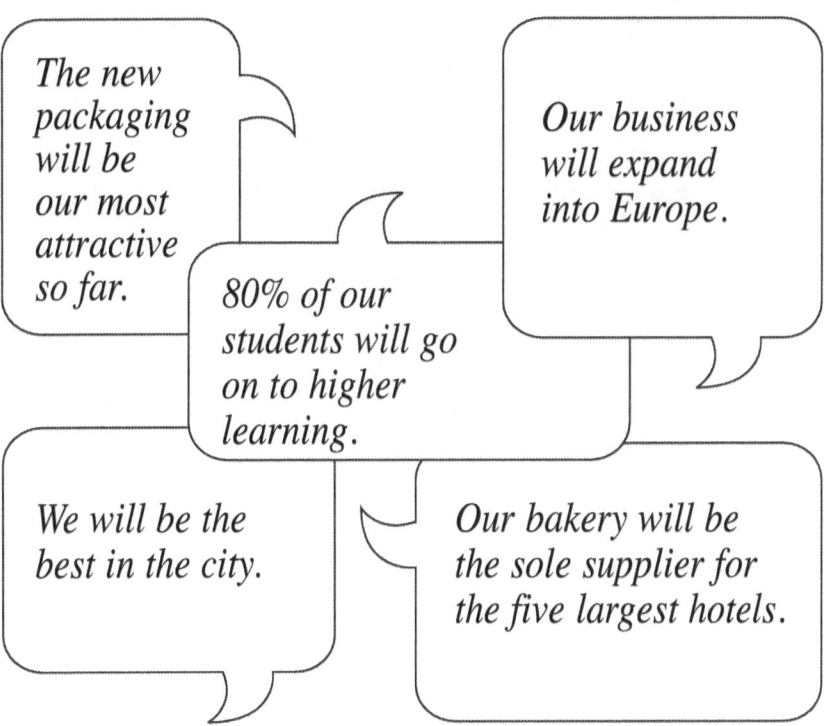

The new packaging will be our most attractive so far.

Our business will expand into Europe.

80% of our students will go on to higher learning.

We will be the best in the city.

Our bakery will be the sole supplier for the five largest hotels.

Vision is important. Have you seen the vision and mission statements that adorn the walls of corporate North America? They are profound words, agonized over by teams of leaders striving to reduce to a few key phrases the essence of what they want to be known for and how they want their employees to act.

Vision is critical. It's the life blood of change, and change is essential for corporate sustainability and growth. A well-articulated vision energizes the reader and stirs thoughts of possibilities. It makes dreamers of the employees who see new opportunities on the horizon; it promises a break from their routine, perhaps a chance to tackle something new. If it's talked about and discussed, with the view to making it come alive in each and every department, then true growth can and will become evident.

On the other side of the coin are the vision statements that, while produced and plastered on the walls of every office, reduced in size to fit in a wallet or posted on a desk, made into key chains and printed on the back of every business card, are never discussed, explored or considered beyond the visible package of trinkets. The vision in this case is a stand-alone exercise with nothing tangible to show other than the words themselves. This is a hollow example of leaders wanting to show something but not quite sure exactly how to make it meaningful.

Effective leaders will seek opportunities to talk with their employees about the corporate vision and ask, "How can we use those words to create a vision for us in this department, so we can support the corporate one?" Together they develop a strategy, an action plan and find people to champion the goal.

When the leader looks to the vision and asks,

- *How can we make this come alive?*
- *How can we breathe life into it?*
- *What can we do differently or focus on, that will show we are living the vision?*
- *What can we do that will make a difference and move us closer to the vision?*

The vision will spring to life in people's minds and generate all sorts of notions and ideas. Ultimately it will generate a momentum all its own, it will enable people to move forward with clarity.

I was reminded of this the other day when I was driving past a lake where the Canadian National Rowing Team practices. It was shrouded in fog and I couldn't even see the dock and the boathouse. There were no sculls out on the water as they could not see far enough to row with confidence and speed without the possibility of hitting something or each other. The lack of vision stalled the action. It's sometimes like that at work too. Without a true sense of where they should be heading, employees slow down or are completely stalled. Vision is important. It's about hope, passion, dreams and energy. Vision takes the ordinary every day tasks and makes them into special activities that propel people to make outstanding progress.

The challenge then, is for the leader, who may or may not have been involved in the creation of the vision, to take the words and help his employees see value in making them their own.

First and foremost the leader has to believe in the vision, because his or her next job is to embrace it, live it and make it part and parcel of everything they do. Only by bringing it into their work life can they truly expect others to do likewise. This may not be easy – the leader may be skeptical at first, may not see how it can make a difference in the day-to-day routine, or why the effort involved is worth what may end up being a very small pay off.

Vision is like showing someone the happy, cheering, back-slapping team at the finish line then systematically plotting a course of action to achieve that end. When the leaders in the organization can "see" the end, give everyone an oar, the knowledge and skills to row, then push them from shore, they have created and acted upon vision.

However small the action or tentative the movement, the momentum created by even one or two is astonishing. True, there will be some who don't row; they just want to sit in the boat and come along for the ride. However, the magic of team synergy can be immensely energizing and some who initially "sat it out," will join the effort.

A story about Vision

A dancer in a well-known performing arts academy was interested in securing a coveted position in a special performance.

Her dance coach wondered how badly she wanted to perform in this routine and, when told of its importance asked if she could visualize herself dancing on stage on opening night. The dancer said "no" since she was too concerned right now with just passing the audition.

The coach realized that if the dancer could not imagine being successful, there was a strong possibility she would be disappointed at the audition. He asked the dancer if she'd be willing to combine her practice time with some time reflecting on what it would be like to realize her vision. The dancer was skeptical but agreed to follow his plan.

With auditions just one week away the young dancer practiced her routine for hours at a time. At the beginning of each session the coach asked her to sit quietly and imagine herself on stage, dressed in costume, dancing like she'd never danced before, full of confidence, grace and poise. He asked her to feel the warmth from the footlights, to hear the music flowing from the orchestra, to see herself move on to the stage and to dance through her routine, to hear the applause, to see herself bowing, to smile when she accepted the bouquet of flowers, to smell their fragrance. This quiet meditative time was followed by practices during which the coach noted a change in the young dancer. She looked and acted more like a star. She exuded confidence. She smiled more often, she relaxed.

The day came for the auditions and the dancer and coach met outside the door to the stage. The coach said, "Remember your vision – see yourself dancing, hear the audience clapping, feel the pride."

The young dancer went on stage and danced like never before and wowed the adjudicators. On the actual night of the performance she moved through the steps with poise and confidence and was rewarded with thundering applause.

Afterwards, she said how important it had been to "see the end result" in her mind and how that vision had sustained her when doubts crept in.

heatherconsults@shaw.ca **L** is for Leader

Watching

To observe, to be spectator, to take a professional or private interest, be vigilant, protecting care over, look out for.

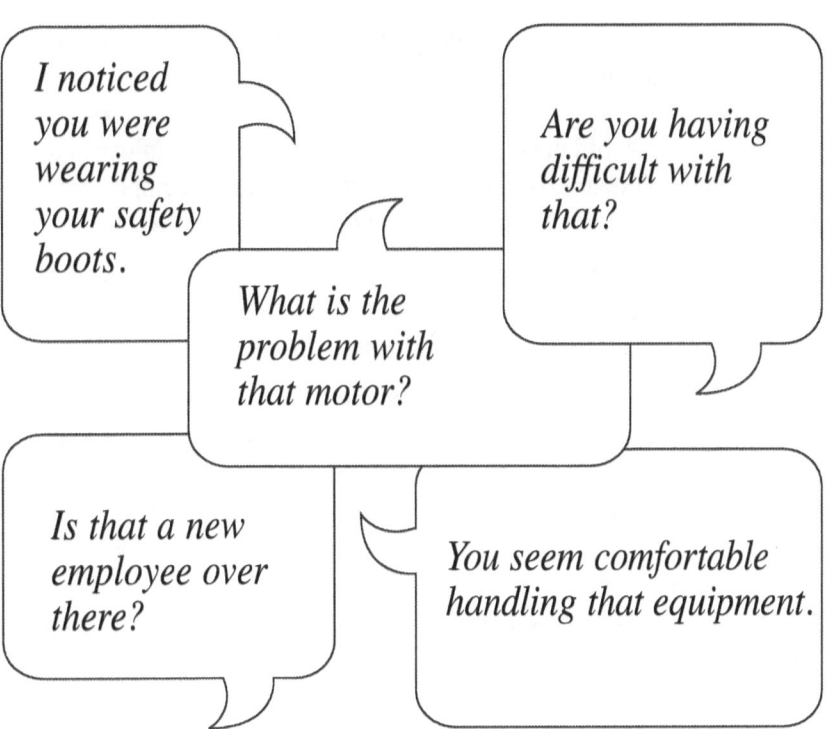

I noticed you were wearing your safety boots.

Are you having difficult with that?

What is the problem with that motor?

Is that a new employee over there?

You seem comfortable handling that equipment.

When a trainer was explaining that the role of supervision had changed from the "good old days," and that employees now considered it normal to be included in planning and to make many of the day-to-day decisions I silently applauded. He went on to say supervision is not really about "super vision," as in the old days when a supervisor watched closely to make sure employees did as they were told. In those days it was more like spying to make sure the employees were following the rules to the letter; something like a cop on patrol.

In the past employees were much more submissive and timid about speaking out, in case it jeopardized their job. And in general they believed they were lucky to be working and that no matter what, their boss was to be respected. These employees were prepared to suffer a bit in order to bring home the paycheck.

Nowadays, instead of being out watching for employee errors, it's much more likely that you'd find the supervisor busy with paperwork in an office far removed from the actual production taking place on a shop floor.

In this case the pendulum has swung in the other direction and leaders are often too far removed from the work, to the extent that they are no longer able to catch the small things that really need their prompt intervention. This, of course, means they depend on the employees to pay close attention, to take the initiative, to show they're empowered to act by making the various calls to deal with things as they arise.

However, encouraging a more watchful style doesn't always bring about the desired results, because people don't always see the important, or right, things, because people notice different things.

If you take a group of about 15 – 20 people and ask them to identify what they first noticed when they entered the room you'll find about half will say they noticed "things" while the other half will tell you they noticed "people." Taken further, if you ask leaders to walk with you around the office or shop floor some leaders unconsciously notice the myriad of things that can potentially go wrong, the mistakes and the problems, while others seem to zero in on the outstanding work being accomplished.

Effective leaders need to cultivate an ability to do both. People need to train themselves to see the whole picture and not just the parts. The lazy way we watch can be explained by a simple workshop question. Half-way through a full-day workshop with 20 participants I asked everyone to look at the ceiling. Then while their heads were facing upwards, I asked, *"What color is the carpet?" **Only one person knew!*** Clearly we don't pay attention even though we appear to be watching.

The police officer driving down a street will notice far more than the average person as their training requires them to give a running commentary of what they notice as they are driving. It's recognized that being highly observant is a crucial skill for their profession.

Research shows that leaders who spend some time consciously "watching" employees find it extremely valuable. When they are able to "see what is going on" they are in a better position to ask about problem situations, provide feedback on the things that are working and those that need fine-tuning. Importantly, these interactions are crucial for both high morale and exceptional quality.

Staying connected is what's really happening; being present, visible and accessible are key to forming relationships and it is strong relationships that build cooperation and collaboration with all of the give and take required to get work done. The chair pulled up to join a group over coffee will go a long way to build bridges and enable the leader to learn about the people behind the work. One manager I knew started a brown bag lunch event each Friday. It was a come-if-you-can event, which grew over time and led to mini lunch 'n learn sessions.

Yet the business of the day-to-day paperwork, meetings, emails and consultations with others, quickly erodes the time many leaders would like to spend with their staff. Making time for connecting with employees – walking around the shop floor, stopping to observe an interaction with a customer and applying focused watching – will reveal all manner of facts enabling leaders to converse with employees so that mutual learning takes place. Clearly this is an important management task.

A story about Watching

A huge industrial operation was suffering some labor unrest and a full-scale strike was underway. As one of a team of consultants, brought in to interview employees to find out exactly what the issues were, I met and spoke with a number of people throughout the plant.

Interviews were scheduled and employees agreed to come into the operation to talk with the consultants and air their concerns. At the end of each day the consultants met over dinner to talk about their findings. Over time some patterns emerged, warranting further, more involved, conversations. It became increasingly obvious that one section of this operation had happier, more content employees than most others. Clearly something was happening that was not immediately apparent.

On one particular day interviews were being held with the middle management team and one of the opening approaches was to ask the individual to walk us through the first hour of their day at work. We'd say, *"On a typical day, tell us what you do after you park your car."* Many of these managers told of a quick cup of coffee, picking up mail, checking their "in basket," going over their email, rushing for the morning meeting, etc. All fairly normal and predictable things for someone in that position.

There was one exception. One manager told us that after he parked his car he "popped down to the shop floor to check in with the employees." We asked, what does "check in"' mean? He then told us he walked through the plant and if he noticed anything that seemed amiss he stopped to see what the employees needed from him. If he could, he'd provide the help right away. He mentioned that just yesterday he'd seen a new employee sweeping up another colleagues work area and as it wasn't part of his job, he was able to say thanks for helping out. He also told us about a new packaging system that was damaging the product, and how he needed to see how things were progressing. And he explained how he had an employee whose wife was in hospital and he wanted to find out how he was managing with the kids. We asked him how often he did this and he told us it was how he started every day. This was, of course, the department, with the employees who reported most favorably about both the work and their manager.

heatherconsults@shaw.ca **L is for Leader**

We asked the manager how long he spent on the floor each morning and he said "between 30 minutes to an hour at the most."

We then asked the other managers about this variation from the pattern exhibited by the majority. They commented that they wished they had the time to connect with their employees, but all of the administrative things consumed their day. We noted their employees seldom, if ever, received any verbal feedback on their performance and during our interviews had told us they felt neglected. "Our supervisor never comes down on the floor to see what we're doing" was a common remark we'd heard during our conversations.

Further exploration surfaced some interesting things about the paperwork and emails these managers were dealing with. Almost 30% came from their own employees who, not seeing their manager face-to-face, had to resort to memos and emails to get production or maintenance issues resolved.

Given that only one manager in this entire operation made any effort to connect with employees it was quite apparent why there was so much hostility, anger and labor strife. The effort it took to bring both sides together spanned several years, with hundreds of hours devoted to building leadership skills that had never been acquired, were rusty from lack of use or had been totally ignored for so long they were no longer even remembered.

ABC
DEFG
HIJK
LMNO
PQRS
TUVW
XYZ

etraordinary

Out of the usual course, exceptional,
surprising usually great.

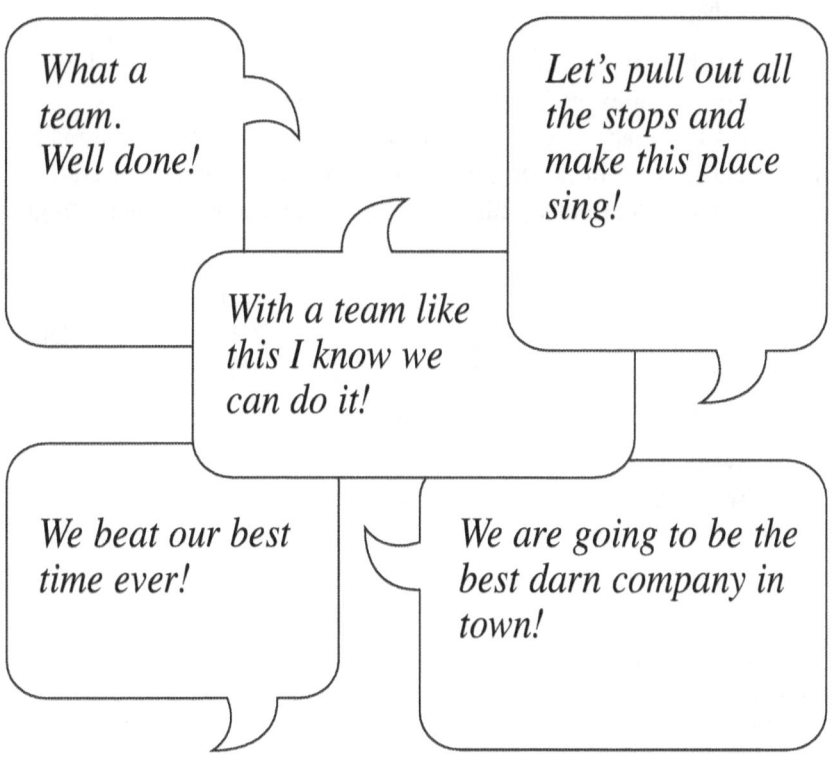

> *What a team. Well done!*

> *Let's pull out all the stops and make this place sing!*

> *With a team like this I know we can do it!*

> *We beat our best time ever!*

> *We are going to be the best darn company in town!*

Xtraordinary results must be the goal for every leader. You've heard it before; accepting "good" is the nail in the coffin of "great" or "outstanding!"

Being complacent, and accepting that when the results are good there's no need to sweat the small stuff, only means that in time good will have slipped to mediocre, substandard or, worse still, totally unacceptable.

The people who stay in business want more, much more than "good." They want:

- **outstanding**
- **extraordinary**
- **amazing** and
- **astonishing results**

They want something that makes you sit up and pay attention like never before. These business leaders know that being complacent will be the death knoll of their operation as their competition is constantly striving to outdo them.

The idea behind providing extraordinary service is to offer a product or service that far exceeds the client's or customer's expectations, something that makes them say, "wow." The type of surprise that makes them want to come back for more, to seek you out when they need more exemplary service; to talk with family and friends about the place to go for great service or products.

Getting employees to be passionate about what they do and getting them fired up and enthusiastic is another matter. What do these leaders do to create the energy, the motivation and the thrill of the action that spurs people to create such amazing results?

It starts with "vision," seeing the possibilities and being passionate about "what can be." Creating a concrete, tangible vision, which you can "sell" to others is crucial. The leader must be able to "see" the end result, know what it will look like and derive a great deal of excitement about bringing the team on side.

The leader cannot expect employees to be thrilled about something that they portray as just a simple notch up of their regular service. The leader has to think BIG and act as if it's entirely possible, attainable, manageable, so others will believe that their combined effort will pull it off, regardless of what "it" is.

The leader who can instill in his or her employees an enthusiasm for the work ahead is more than half way there. Once the energy and enthusiasm is present, all manner of things will occur to make it happen. Employees will be creative, offer ideas and solutions, discuss and remedy stumbling blocks, and take on additional work with the goal of making a real difference.

Energy and enthusiasm is contagious. Think back and recall some service you've had, both the good and the bad.

Have you ever been served by someone who clearly doesn't give a damn, someone who has lost interest, who is tired of the humdrum repetitiveness of it all? Now think about a time when you were served by someone who seemed to be having a good time; someone who was happy, laughing, and pulling out all the stops to make sure you were taken care of.

Most people can easily remember how they felt in similar instances. Perhaps you can too. In one instance you may have felt only too pleased to leave, while in another you may well have chatted with the employee and stayed longer than originally intended. Research shows that people who like doing their work tend to have some of that joy rub off on those around them, whether that's colleagues or customers or suppliers.

The effective leader who wants extraordinary results must exhibit an enthusiasm and belief in the work being done and the people doing it.

They constantly ask:
- *What more can we do?*
- *How else can we make a difference to our customers?*
- *What's in the way?*
- *How can we remove obstacles?*

Ordinary people who believe they can do extraordinary work produce extraordinary results.

Effective leaders generally find ways to support their employees and remove obstacles and barriers. In other words, they point the way, provide the resources and clear away the obstructions. These leaders operate in an "I want to be in service to my employees" mindset.

A story about eXtraordinary

In the winter of *1996* a major blizzard hit Victoria, BC, a place where winter seldom comes as it does to the rest of Canada. Known for its mild and balmy winters, the snow that fell in late December threatened to play havoc with the travel plans of many family members. The other side of this potential catastrophe was the opportunity for young and old alike to play, take photographs, stay indoors and watch the snow fall, or bundle up and build snowmen, toss snowballs, make snow forts and enjoy the silence as the city was wrapped in a thick, white blanket.

The snow fell, and fell and fell. Day and night is snowed and the magical image of the picnic table with six inches of snow turned to "where is the picnic table?" It became apparent that the city was gripped in a layer of white that restricted, if not completed eliminated, movement of any transportation.

At this point a local radio station was flooded with calls. People on the coast had been told that in the event of an earthquake to turn on their radio for information, now in the snowstorm, they did the same. The radio station quickly realized they were being looked to, to help the citizens find help.

Over the next five days the radio broadcast non-stop and linked people and services from all over the city. A doctor who needed to get to the hospital was linked to someone who had a snowmobile. A mother in labor was linked to a midwife in her neighborhood who skied to deliver the baby. An elderly person who needed medication was linked to a pharmacy that was open and then linked to someone who could pick up and deliver the medication. Hour after hour calls came in for help and people in a position to provide assistance came forward.

Whole neighborhoods pitched in to help. They called in to offer what transportation, knowledge or skills they had to assist their fellow citizens and the radio station kept on advising and linking people. People walked and skied to the few shops that were open to get food and help their neighbours. One radio station employee skied over 16 kilometers to relieve the employees who had been marooned in the station since the start of the storm.

In the end, when life went back to normal, the radio station received an award for its outstanding community service. Clearly the employees who worked there rose to the occasion and provided a service which was truly a lifeline to many throughout the city. This is one example of eXtraordinary service from eXtraordinary citizens!

ABC
DEFG
HIJK
LMNO
PQRS
TUVW
XYZ

Yes

To express agreement, consent, affirmation; used to express interest and as an invitation to say more.

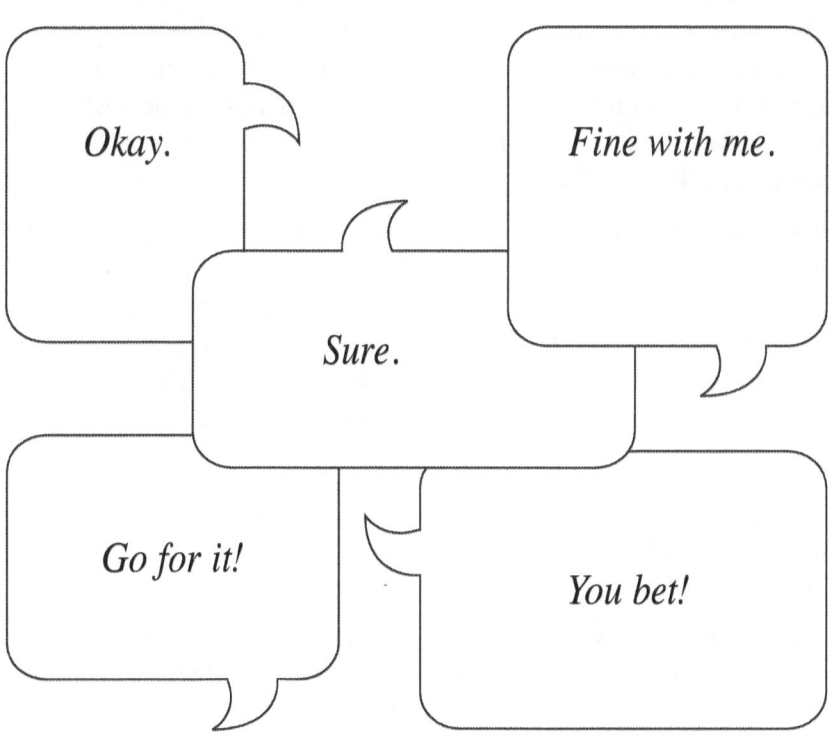

Okay.

Fine with me.

Sure.

Go for it!

You bet!

Yes, you may have heard it before, but it's worth repeating: *"It's easier to ask for forgiveness than to get permission?"*

So many leaders are anxious about making a mistake that they don't take the actions necessary for the business to grow and thrive. Sometimes they don't even make decisions that are clearly in the best interests of the employees and their customers for fear that they may not stand the test of time.

It's easy to say, *"No"* to something that is new, was tried once and proved unsuccessful, or doesn't appear to be endorsed by existing policies or procedures.

However, progress requires moves into the unknown, untested, unproven arena. Yet this same change, which could be so invigorating, often leaves people feeling vulnerable, and insecure. They worry about foul-ups and lack of support so that they, in essence, become paralyzed and retreat to the same habitual patterns and known procedures.

The leader who is willing to go slowly, to consider anxieties, to pause and consider the possibility of heading in a new direction is frequently rewarded, as over time employees bring forward ideas for new ways to save funds, create new products, or discover alternative approaches to service clients.

The leader who is able to say *"why don't you try it," "check it out and bring us some more details,"* or *"sounds good to me,"* demonstrates a willingness to explore untested approaches and take some risks. The leader who takes risks shows the employees that making a few mistakes is completely acceptable in the world of business growth. That fine-tuning and course correction is a normal and acceptable part of any business endeavor; that errors create learning and expands capabilities.

It's important to look at the jobs people perform and consider how long things have been the same and whether they might be ready for a shake up, a fresh approach or an untried avenue.

A willingness to go out on a limb does not mean you need recklessly abandon sound business practices. A responsible risk assessment should be part of every major shift and a change should only be undertaken after all significant risks have been minimized. Accepting that not

heatherconsults@shaw.ca **L is for Leader**

everything you start will survive, or that everything you plan will work out, is also important to acknowledge and discuss with your staff. The leader has to know when to abandon something and cut the losses; and doing so must be an option, as stalling or slowing something down often allows time to reassess and regroup.

The leader who wants innovation, risk taking and courage to become the way of life must make sure employees know they will be buffered from any negative ramifications and finger pointing. The leader must stand behind the employees and defend their actions and help them recover from any setbacks.

The leader in every organization, in just about every corner of the globe, is facing changes like never before and this is showing no sign of slowing down. Each new initiative jump-starts another and the ripple effect cascades beyond the industry where the seed of change originated. Change is not always an idea, a dream in the mind of an employee, a desire to create; sometimes it's in reaction to what is happening in other parts of the organization, industry or country.

The wise leader looks at the circumstances, the facts, the risks and, whenever possible, seeks to find a way to endorse the venture so that the building blocks of growth and innovation stay alive. Say "yes" whenever you can.

A story about Yes

A management and training consultant who made a career shift and started to operate a small farm as a pre-retirement project found the venture far more demanding than originally anticipated. In addition some significant issues surfaced which meant that the dream of becoming a self-sufficient farmer had to be reassessed.

She consulted a colleague from her training and organizational development days, to gain a fresh new perspective on her dilemma. He suggested she take her training and education background and apply it to her farm by creating an education center on organic farming.

They mulled over all sorts of ideas, assessed the risks and, as the "farmer/consultant" was an innovative and energetic risk-taker, she plunged ahead. She said "Yes."

Brochures were created, teachers were contacted and in no time school busses were arriving full of grade school children ready for their tours. The Alpacas were petted, the vegetables were sampled, the weeds were pulled, and the flowers were picked by young students who, in many cases, had never thought about how farmers did their work. Month after month the children arrived and came back on the weekends pulling Mum or Dad up the driveway to show them "their farm."

Yet in spite of saying "Yes" to this venture and in spite of getting the great response to the tours, the "farmer" found she was unable to keep up with her expanded, not redirected role.

Now she had to be both farmer AND tour guide and the farm was suffering from her lack of attention. This in turn caused fewer people to visit. So yet another path proved to be a dead end.

In time the "farmer" abandoned her pre-retirement plan and went back to her consulting work. When asked, she tells people that, "saying yes to the farming venture wasn't a mistake." She adds, *"I learned a lot about myself my capabilities and the whole world of farming life opened my eyes to things I'd taken for granted."* She often tells people, *"I'm glad I tried it. If I hadn't I would have always wondered if I should have gone along that path. The person I am today would not exist if it hadn't been for those years. I'm glad I took that route, hard as it was."*

heatherconsults@shaw.ca **L is for Leader**

Zeal

Earnestness, passion in advancing a cause, or rendering a service; hearty and persistent endeavor.

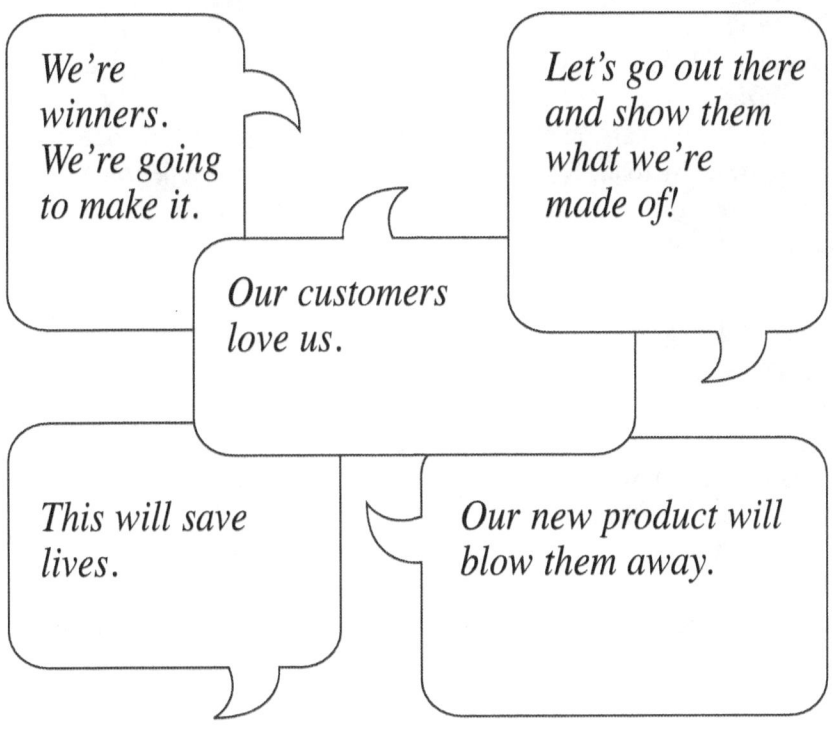

We're winners. We're going to make it.

Let's go out there and show them what we're made of!

Our customers love us.

This will save lives.

Our new product will blow them away.

*Z*ealous employees can be exhausting. Yet, when leaders are fortunate enough to have an employee, whose energy and enthusiasm seems to have no bounds and energizes them so they take on extraordinary challenges, it can be exhilarating and draining at the same time, wonderful and challenging, easy and hair-raising.

The passion, the drive, the endless energy can leave others tired just from watching them steam ahead! Yet this energy and passion, for a cause, a project or a new venture, can have a stimulating impact on others who frequently get swept up in their vision.

The wise and experienced leader will know when to stay out of the limelight and let the employee steer the activities, to own the work at hand. It's also important to recognize when it's time to step in, to caution the employee and remind them that not everyone can or wants to make such sweeping overtures, to ride the wave of activity as they do. The zealous employee or enthusiastic leader may feel their colleagues lack initiative or are unmotivated, whereas they may simply pursue things in a quieter manner.

The zeal, the boundless enthusiasm and the drive to excel, which is so often lacking in the workplace, can be a breath of fresh air in an organization preoccupied with policies, procedures and a consistent routine. Yet the passion for some aspect of the work generally needs to be followed by routine, stable steps to bring the plan to a dependable conclusion. This daily slog with routine tasks can be where the energy and passion of the creative person can diminish.

A young man, I knew, had a dream of becoming a commercial pilot, when at the age eleven he joined air cadets. He held on to that goal and worked at it over the next nine years. Flying was his passion – it was how he spent his free time and how he used any money he had at his disposal. In the summer of his fifteenth year he received his glider's license and then when he was eighteen he obtained his pilot's license. In order to get into the air force, which was his dream job, he needed to improve his marks. When he left school he took a part-time job and attended college to upgrade in some areas and improve his chances of being accepted. He went through a round of interviews and sadly was not accepted into Royal Military College as hoped. Undeterred he signed up for flight training at a college away from home, so he'd be ready to try again the following year. This young man knew what he wanted, was passionate about his dream and could see himself there in the captain's seat. When he struggled with the slog work that was necessary to make his dream a reality his mother stepped in and reminded him of the end result and encouraged him not to give up. It was just the kind of nudging he needed to stay the course.

So, it's during the routine work, following the early creative, brain-storming stage that the leader often finds they need to provide support.

Managing the peaks and valleys of energy can, at times, be like handling a time bomb – enthusiasm one minute, with a commitment to stay the course and get the work done, followed by a disruptive often dragging of heels over the routine tasks, that however dull, are needed to bring things to completion.

The effective leader knows that the passion and energy evident at the commencement of any new and exciting project will diminish over time. Sometimes it's because the work proves to be more challenging than initially anticipated, while at other times it's due to the nature and style of the players. Blending the creative, energetic style of some with the detail-oriented, meticulous style of others will certainly make things more stable without diluting the drive to make a difference.

The wise leader will generally allow an energetic and enthusiastic team to forge ahead with minimal interference, as long as they know the boundaries, have specific goals and understand they must uphold the values of the organization.

So what about the situation when the leader is passionate about something but the employees are reluctant to embrace things to the same degree? How can the leader stir up the troops and inspire them to reach for the gold?

Perhaps you are full of enthusiasm, walk with a jaunty step, and exude a positive attitude. If so I can almost guarantee your employees will line up to follow wherever you may lead. People want to march behind the drummer who plays a striking tempo. In general, the leaders most admired, are active, energetic, enthusiastic, and full of life and passion.

However, you will have to consider the gains to be made from your passion and vision, not only for the organization but also for the employees.

- What's in it for them?
- How will it make their work life more fun, more rewarding, more satisfying?
- How can you "sell" your idea?
- Who will gain from the employee's efforts?
- Will it make them proud to have made a difference?
- What will it take to get them passionate about it too?

The leader will want to show that he or she has identified the "wins" for the organization and the employees too. Make a list of the potential gains and be ready to ask others to join in the venture.

Effective leaders find or support something to get excited about, something important, to add zip, zing, and zeal to the working world. They acknowledge that many of the tasks employees engage in are simply a stream of repetitive, routine activities. But while many employees don't want sweeping change, a bit of variety is generally well accepted.

Look for a cause outside of the work world if necessary, something to add a bit of zest to life, something the employees can do that will give them variety and a sense of pride by making a difference. Examples might include locating a family in need, donating blood, or a run, walk or bike for an important cause. Perhaps the employees can establish a company choir to entertain local seniors, have a marathon knitting event to make blankets for the homeless, "adopt" a family for Christmas and create a hamper and gifts for them. The ideas are endless.

The idea is to ensure that there is something to generate excitement and enthusiasm so people can rally around something important.

A story about Zeal

Every year groups of employees in a large government office situated in a large sprawling metropolis "adopt" families who have been brought to their attention through social agencies, the police, the hospital or the fire department.

One group of employees wanted to do something new, refreshing and exciting to make an impact in a totally different manner. They didn't want to become yet another group giving the traditional hamper or gifts to a family; they wanted to make a longer term impact on these people's lives, and encourage them to "pass the baton" so to speak. They talked over the possibilities and brainstormed with others in the company and finally an idea was formed.

They devised a plan to work *with* the family. The employees invited the family to visit their worksite and meet the team. Some employees took the children shopping to buy gifts for their Mum or Dad. Some went shopping with the mother to help her select her own food items and find a small treasure for her husband, while some of the others took Dad to get a tree and a small gift for his wife. Then the employees took over the boardroom and had a craft day with their "adopted" children, making decorations and cards. They also invited their "adopted" family to join them at their company party.

The relationship they formed with the family took root and in time led to unforeseen gains when the youngest daughter was hired to join the company on a short-term project to gain some skills. Her shy manner had hindered her from seeking employment in places full of strangers but in this organization she was "one of the family" and her quiet style was not seen as unusual or an impediment.

The following year the employees invited this first family to join them with their new adopted family. They were included in the shopping, in making crafts, in selecting a tree, baking cookies and other treats and they thoroughly enjoyed the experience of giving to others.

Now, some five years later, the initial family is following the example of those few employees by going out and making a contribution to others in their own community. Truly the baton is being passed from employees to families and far beyond and it all stemmed from some enthusiastic and zealous employees who saw an opportunity and found a way to bring it to reality.

ABC
DEFG
HIJK
LMNO
PQRS
TUVW
XYZ

Summary

Leading for success

This book has covered some of the main teachings and lessons from highly effective leaders. But like all sources of information, whether it's from a book, workshop facilitator, college instructor, mentor, coach, or colleague, it will mean nothing if it's not taken, considered, and fully integrated into your life.

You've heard it before; when supervisors and managers head off to leadership workshops the employees wait for them to return from "charm school," to see what they're going to try out on them. The wise leader, however, will set aside some time to share with the employees some of the things they learned. They share the stories, examples and things they gleaned from other participants. Specifically, they discuss what they'd like to improve on and what they will be making a concerted effort to apply in the coming weeks.

The employees faced with this information no longer needs to question what's going on when their leader behaves in a different manner. It is transparent and clear that their leader is working on the skills he or she told them they were trying to develop. This also enables the employees to work with their leader and to provide some feedback on how the changes have affected them.

There's no question that it takes courage to do things differently; in general, we are creatures of habit, settled and comfortable in our old ways – even if they don't serve us very well.

So if change is important to you, and if skill development is crucial for you to operate at your optimum level, you may want to consider using some of the templates in the Appendix.

They are provided so you can complete some self-assessments on key leadership areas. The information will serve you in moving forward to expand your knowledge and skills so you can develop stronger working relationships.

Please use the materials with care. Answer these questions when you are experiencing a fairly normal, routine day, because the way in which you answer these questions will depend on how you feel at the time.

On a day when everything has progressed smoothly you will easily remember the leadership behaviors that have served you well, while on a day fraught with problems you may end up feeling you are a hopeless leader. In reality you are probably somewhere in between.

Sometimes a courageous leader will ask employees to answer similar questions to those in the Appendix, to obtain a different perspective on his or her leadership approach. This will not only provide you with some very useful information but will demonstrate your open and reflective leadership style. It's a rare leader who will pro-actively seek an in-depth perspective of their working style.

However, before you ask for feedback make sure you are ready and willing to act on some of the input. It can be particularly troubling when nothing happens as a result of the employee's information. It can also be somewhat disturbing to employees when the leader's style changes to the point when they are not longer operating in their old established way. Now the employees have to change too, to adapt to the "new" working style, and may not experience the same degree of ease.

In any case, employees are watching, waiting and anxious to see if any changes will be positive, creating a more harmonious and cooperative working relationship.

As a result of completing the templates in the Appendix, you may find many opportunities to adapt your style in order to become a more effective leader, but don't try to do everything at once! Take it easy. Engage in one or two approaches and strive to perfect them before heading on to something else.

In responding to some of the assessment questions, you may be surprised to find you are already operating as an effective leader. If that should be the case, give yourself a well-deserved pat on the back and then ask yourself, "Is better possible?" Leaders everywhere are adapting in response to organizational changes, market conditions, global impact, personnel changes and their own learning. Learning and leading is a continuous process, by picking up "L is for Leader" you have started on your own leadership adventure.

I hope that this book has given you some insight into the many faces of leadership and inspired you to take the next step to becoming the leader you were always meant to be.

For consultation, workshops or coaching contact:

Heather Hughes, Management Consultant, Author and Leadership Coach
HH and *Your* Company
Telephone: 1- 250-708-0464 or 1- 250-812-5833
E-mail: heatherconsults@shaw.ca

One of the best web sites for leaders and coaches that I know of is:
www.peer.ca I encourage you to check it out!

ABC
DEFG
HIJK
LMNO
PQRS
TUVW
XYZ

Appendices

Establishing a Vision So Employees Can Focus Their Efforts

This template will provide an opportunity for you to *establish vision* and *provide a focus* for the people who report to you.

To what extent have you:	not yet	seldom	sometimes	regularly
developed and communicated the purpose and strategies of the organization?				
asked for ideas, suggestions and input into the process of developing vision, strategies, purpose and objectives?				
identified clear business objectives to fulfil the purpose and strategies of the organization?				
made sure measures were developed to identify how well objectives are being met?				
explained to others how they can influence the results of the organization?				
ensured that personal performance objectives have been set and measures have been established?				
identified and then described the value in achieving the results?				
identified the "high leverage" opportunities for improvement?				
identified what's required for everyone in the organization to work together effectively and respectfully?				
created and communicated guiding principles for working together effectively?				

If you marked "not yet," please consider and record some next steps for you and your people.

If you marked "regularly," please ensure that your experience is passed on for others to benefit within your organization.

Hiring

This template provides an opportunity for you to examine the work you have engaged in to **retain the right people**.

To what extent have you:	not yet	seldom	sometimes	regularly
identified the competencies required for each position?				
ensured everyone understood what competencies are required for their position?				
followed an effective and proven selection process?				
been involved with team members in the selection process?				
trained team members in the selection process?				
spent time continually evaluating the effectiveness of the selection process?				
tracked the performance and overall success of new employees?				
asked employees, who experienced the selection process, for their feedback?				
updated and improved the selection process?				
set up a process for continuously evaluating everyone's performance?				
ensured that panel interviews are conducted and that 4–5 names have been provided for reference checking?				
made sure that candidates are rated immediately following the interview while the panel is still in place and information is fresh?				
made sure that the team reaches consensus on the score for each applicant?				
identified 2–3 applicants who passed both the testing and the interview, prior to reference checking?				

continued on page 163

To what extent have you:	not yet	seldom	sometimes	regularly
made sure that all reference checks must be good in all areas and cover: confirmation of dates of employment, positions held, why the employee left, responsibility, attitude, and relationships with others, strong and weak points?				
conducted fitness testing, using an independent company, and requested medical tests?				
brought the candidate in for pre-employment training and orientation and given them time with the other employees?				
made a formal offer of employment to the successful candidate? and upon acceptance, informed the unsuccessful candidates?				

If you marked "not yet," please consider and record some next steps for you and your people.

If you marked "regularly," please ensure that your experience is passed on for others so they can benefit from your experience.

Design a Process that Facilitates Change

This area provides an opportunity for you to consider what you have done to **design a process that facilitates change.**

To what extent have you:	not yet	seldom	sometimes	regularly
involved others in identifying the need for change or improvement?				
explained the forces that have an impact on the organization – internal, external, current and those anticipated?				
evaluated how your processes and results compared to what others are doing?				
identified and communicated the value of changing?				
built credibility for change leadership, i.e. have you delivered what you said you would?				
responded quickly to ideas, suggestions and concerns?				
created visible changes, i.e. sprucing up the place, as a symbol of change?				
increased communication, so you tell them everything?				
been visible, out talking with people to find out about their concerns and excitement?				
taken action to address the concerns and build on the excitement?				
put in place resources, systems and structures to enable changes to take place?				
helped to reorganize the work loads or created ways to allow time so people can focus on change initiatives?				
recognized and rewarded people for engaging in change and improvement activities?				

If you marked "not yet," please consider and record some next steps for you and your people.

If you marked "regularly," please ensure that your experience is passed on for others to benefit.

Track And Understand Results

This area provides an opportunity for you to consider what
you have engaged in to **track and understand results**.

To what extent have you:	not yet	seldom	sometimes	regularly
explained to others the value in tracking individual and team performance?				
identified and developed measures for each of the "critical performance factors?"				
developed a tracking system that is timely, easy to use, highly visible and accurate?				
identified and set targets for results, and benchmarked other organizations?				
measured your performance and tracked results?				
reviewed results with team members?				
taken preventative or corrective action based on the results?				
reset the targets for continuous improvement?				
challenged people to improve performance and achieve better results?				

If you marked "not yet," please consider and record
some next steps for you and your people.

If you marked "regularly," please ensure that your
experience is passed on for others to benefit.

Build Involvement and Partnerships

This area provides an opportunity for you to consider the work you have engaged in to **build involvement** and **partnerships**.

To what extent have you:	not yet	seldom	sometimes	regularly
included others and shared information with them regarding your business, your customers, the priorities and challenges and the organizational structure?				
developed goals collaboratively, with your supervisors, subordinates and peers?				
communicated your expectations and asked others what they expect of you?				
listened to and respected each other's expectations?				
agreed together on which expectations you will meet and which ones you're unwilling to meet?				
pitched in to get the job done, no matter what it took and no matter what your role was?				
made an effort to learn other people's jobs so you understood how your performance affects their jobs and how you can help them?				
figured out what needed to be done then went ahead and did it? invited others to contribute to making decisions that affect the business?				
immediately disclosed concerns you had with a working relationship and took appropriate measures to resolve the issues?				
regularly asked, "How well are we working together? How can we improve our relationship?"				

If you marked "not yet," please consider and record some next steps for you and your people.

If you marked "regularly," please ensure that your experience is passed on so others benefit.

Provide Understanding and Skill Development

This area provides an opportunity for you to look at the work
you have engaged in to **provide understanding** and
skill development for your department.

To what extent have you:	not yet	seldom	sometimes	regularly
been involved in communicating an understanding of the business to others, i.e. customer service, product quality, supply and demand, production and costs, core businesses and financial statements?				
identified technical, managerial, interpersonal and team skills requirements? (E.g. problem solving, decision making, leadership, communication)				
discussed with others the expected outcomes of coaching, training, and development?				
assessed the effectiveness of coaching, training and development and provided feedback and followed up appropriately?				
provided opportunities for others to apply their new skills?				
clearly demonstrated that training and development is important by arranging for job rotation, cross training, and pay for skills, etc?				
made sure that people were aware that they are expected to apply the training and knowledge they gained?				

If you marked "not yet," please consider and record
some next steps for you and your people.

If you marked "regularly," please ensure that your
experience is passed on so others benefit.

Empowerment – Create Opportunities Then Get Out of the Way

This area provides an opportunity for you to look at the work you have engaged in that creates **empowerment** and **finds you getting out of the way** of your people.

To what extent have you:	not yet	seldom	sometimes	regularly
created challenges for your people?				
described and discussed the boundaries of projects and assignments, i.e. budgets, resources, time frames, milestones, checkpoints?				
provided the resources for people to do their jobs?				
provided direction when asked to help, clarified points or answered questions?				
supported and encouraged others so they kept projects moving forward?				
stood back and allowed others to successfully complete projects on their own?				
stepped in only when you are asked for help or a major irreversible disaster was about to occur?				
given others the chance to discover problems on their own and learn from their mistakes?				
given people the authority to carry out their assignments or projects?				
encouraged a de-briefing following a project or assignment to gather information which will help improve things next time?				

If you marked "not yet," please consider and record some next steps for you and your people.

If you marked "regularly," please ensure that your experience is passed on for others to benefit.

heatherconsults@shaw.ca **L is for Leader**

Tell Your Staff Everything and Listen Like Your Life Depends on It.

This area provides an opportunity for you to look at how much you are **telling your employees everything** and **listening all of the time**.

To what extent have you:	not yet	seldom	sometimes	regularly
told people everything about the business both the good and the bad?				
held meetings and "huddles" as often as possible?				
told others how they are performing and given regular feedback?				
asked others about their needs?				
listened to really understand their concerns and questions?				
taken appropriate action in a timely manner to resolve issues and concerns?				
listened to what people need to be more effective doing their job?				
made a point of getting back to people to respond to questions they asked you?				
made it comfortable for others to come forward to make suggestions, ask questions or talk about concerns or complaints?				
held frequent, regular, performance reviews?				

If you marked "not yet," please consider and record some next steps for you and your people.

If you marked "regularly," please ensure that your experience is passed on so others benefit.

Praise, Reward and Recognition

This area provides an opportunity for you to look at the work you have engaged in that finds you **praising, rewarding and recognizing** all of your people for the many contributions they make.

To what extent have you:	not yet	seldom	sometimes	regularly
recognized others for taking calculated risks and for their special efforts?				
said "thanks" in person, written a letter of recognition for your business newsletter, given a gift certificate, or provided a dinner?				
rewarded others for continuous performance improvement efforts, and above-average performance?				
recommended people for promotion, provided salary increases, bonuses, or allowed them to attend conferences or other operations?				
celebrated others successes?				
explained to employees and others how you value their actions?				
identified and talked with "high-performing employees" and helped people see what is valued?				
identified and removed barriers to providing more recognition and rewards?				

If you marked "not yet," please consider and record some next steps for you and your people.

If you marked "regularly," please ensure that your experience is passed on for others to benefit.

Goal Setting Strategic Planning

This area provides an opportunity for you to look at the work you have engaged in that finds you **setting goals to ensure they are aligned with the corporate goals**.

To what extent have you:	not yet	seldom	sometimes	regularly
looked at information, trends and business indicators to assess the constraints and challenges ahead for your employees?				
established priorities for the next quarter?				
involved your people by garnering their input?				
provided all the data so employees see these goals are achievable?				
set objectives with other management levels to ensure alignment?				
asked employees to set their own objectives to ensure they meet the business objectives?				
identified and agreed on resources that you'll provide to help meet those objectives				
met one-on-one, as well as with team members, to make sure objectives are aligned and that everyone knows the goals?				
communicated the goals to anyone who could be affected? i.e. customers, other departments?				
established a tracking system and ensured it is used at least monthly to provide feedback to employees?				
included and discussed group progress at monthly meetings and developed action plans to keep things on track?				
provided recognition to the individuals and teams who have met or exceed expectations?				
met and talked with individuals about their personal objectives and developed action plans with them to address any problems?				

Performance Reviews

This area provides an opportunity for you to assess your work to **clarify expectations, discuss challenges and coach and support employees to higher levels of performance**.

To what extent have you:	not yet	seldom	sometimes	regularly
taken the time to clarify in your own mind what you want each of your employees to do?				
looked at existing job standards, job descriptions, previous appraisals and customer's input?				
considered your performance to see if you have been coaching, supporting and clarifying expectations?				
thought about what you'd like to improve on and how your employees could provide assistance?				
considered that talking about performance is not always a comfortable experience and that you need to create an atmosphere conducive to open dialogue?				
given your employees time to prepare?				
set aside enough time for an open two way discussion that shows the importance of the conversation?				
made sure you are un-interrupted and that your attention is directed to them?				
outlined your expectations and asked them to explain, in their own words, their understanding of what it is you want them to do?				
listened to their concerns, plans or ideas for making these expectations a reality and worked toward agreement with the employee on an action plan?				
determined the major contributions individual employees make to the overall team's effectiveness?				

continued on page 173

To what extent have you:	not yet	seldom	sometimes	regularly
explored why the results were attained and how this knowledge can be used to benefit others?				
talked about what needs to occur for a high level of performance to be attained and maintained?				
discussed the areas where this employee could improve performance and the possible causes for performance being at its present level?				
reached agreement with this employee on an action plan to reach the desired performance?				
considered the role you play in coaching, training, and supporting this employee?				
developed a plan to track results and provide feedback to this employee?				

Business Education

Work in this area indicates a desire to **educate employees on the social, economic** and **technological trends of the business**. It also demonstrates your trust and belief in people, and that armed with accurate up to date information they will make better decisions.

To what extent have you:	not yet	seldom	sometimes	regularly
prepared a presentation covering the basics of the business, using terminology most likely to be understood by employees?				
explained your goals, and operating processes and your key customer's requirements?				
taken the time to explain some of the commonly used terms used in your business so that employees understand more clearly what they mean?				
talked with the employees about how they can affect the results and what their contributions means to the overall productivity of the operation?				
asked the employees to track the results they create and identify ways to make improvements?				
taken steps to ensure key results are presented regularly and that you provide a verbal explanation?				
ensured that regular meetings occur to discuss issues which may affect the business?				
asked your employees what information they would like to see to help them understand the business?				

Developing a Strong Team

Work in this area indicates a commitment to **developing the strongest possible team with the broadest range of skills**. This includes **training, special assignments** and **mentoring and coaching**.

To what extent have you:	not yet	seldom	sometimes	regularly
spent time with each employee to discuss their performance and clarify your expectations?				
worked with your employees to identify skill development opportunities and or training courses to supplement existing expertise?				
contacted Human Resources to find out about "approved" training programs or consultants who can provide the right package for your employees?				
made yourself familiar with the content of any training you are approving for your people?				
met with the employee prior to training to ask them what they aim to get from the course?				
asked the employee to look for opportunities amongst the content and in dialogue with other participants?				
met with the employee within a week of their return, to discuss their experience and the learning that emerged from the training?				
asked them to develop a plan for using some of the lessons and how you might be able to support them?				
followed up to find out how the employee is using the new knowledge or skills?				
encouraged them to bring others up to speed on what they learned?				

Succession Planning

Work in this area indicates an awareness of the need to **plan, develop and retain skilled people within the organization; to promote "high potential" candidates into positions where they can have a significant impact on the company**.

To what extent have you:	not yet	seldom	sometimes	regularly
identified key positions within your department where you want fully qualified internal candidates.				
considered the management style of the existing group and the style you need to complement or balance the group?				
asked for input from your management team on potential employees who could fill that role?				
reviewed the potential candidates with the management team and identified developmental needs for each of the people?				
asked the candidates if they would value the opportunity to develop their skills with the view of filling this role in the future?				
agreed on a development plan with the candidate?				
set clear goals for the development, with timelines for measuring and assessing progress?				
monitored the plan, tracked the results and met regularly with the employee to talk over the results to date?				
identified employees who show potential to move up within the next 3–5 years?				
identified the development required for each high potential candidate?				
met and asked the employee to identify their career aspirations?				

continued on page 177

To what extent have you:	not yet	seldom	sometimes	regularly
drawn up a development plan with the employee?				
taken steps to implement the plan and monitor the results?				
met with the employee to discuss the progress and make modifications as necessary?				
kept a record for future use?				

Personal and Career Development

Work in this area indicates an interest in the **future success of your employees** and in the direction they want their career to take.

To what extent have you:	not yet	seldom	sometimes	regularly
reviewed and noted career plans for each of your employees along with any special interests they have been involved in?				
met with your employees individually to ask about their career plans, as well as current development needs?				
worked with your employees to identify opportunities in the department or within the company where their goals could be met?				
asked your employees what support they would like and agree on what you are willing to offer?				
recorded your understanding of any development opportunities that are to be provided?				
included the development plan in your budget?				
reviewed the progress at least once a year, and whether the career goals are still the same?				
evaluated how effective your development plan is in terms of moving the employee closer to their goal?